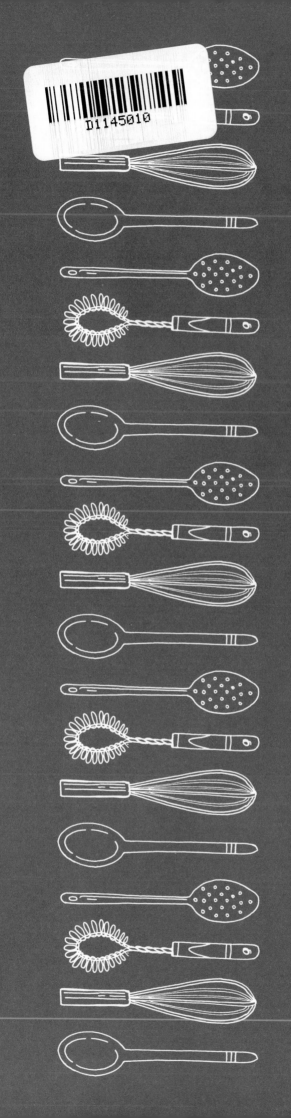

THE DAIRY-FREE COOKBOOK

THE DAIRY-FREE COOKBOOK

OVER 50 DELICIOUS RECIPES THAT
ARE FREE FROM DAIRY PRODUCTS

CONTRIBUTING EDITOR
MAGGIE PANNELL

LORENZ BOOKS

This edition published by Lorenz Books
an imprint of
Anness Publishing Limited
Hermes House
88-89 Blackfriars Road
London SE1 8HA

www.lorenzbooks.com

A CIP catalogue record for this book is available from the British Library

ISBN 1 85967 941 2

Publisher: Joanna Lorenz
Senior Cookery Editor: Linda Fraser
Designer: Ian Sandom
Reader: Felicity Forrester
Photographers: Michelle Garrett and William Lingwood
(Pictures on pp9 and 12 were supplied by Tony Stone Images)
Recipes: Jacqueline Clarke, Carol Clements, Joanna Farrow, Kathy Mann,
Lesley Mackley, Maggie Mayhew and Elizabeth Wolfe-Cohen

Printed and bound in Singapore

© Anness Publishing Limited 1999
Updated © 2000
1 3 5 7 9 10 8 6 4 2

NOTES
For all recipes, quantities are given in both metric and imperial measures
and, where appropriate, measures are also given in standard cups and
spoons. Follow one set, but not a mixture, because they are not
interchangeable.

Standard spoon and cup measures are level.
1 tsp = 5ml, 1 tbsp = 15ml, 1 cup = 250ml/8fl oz

Australian standard tablespoons are 20ml. Australian readers should
use 3 tsp in place of 1 tbsp for measuring small quantities of gelatine,
cornflour, salt, etc.

Medium eggs are used unless otherwise stated.

CONTENTS

INTRODUCTION

Some people choose a dairy-free diet for either moral or religious reasons, but others have the decision made for them when they develop an intolerance or an allergy to cow's milk. Whatever your reason for omitting cow's milk and its products from your diet, you can still enjoy a wide range of varied and delicious meals. All it takes is a little planning. This cookbook is designed to give you all the help, advice and information you need, plus lots of tasty dairy-free recipes for you, your friends and family to enjoy, from soups and starters to main courses, desserts, cakes and bakes.

WHAT EXACTLY ARE DAIRY FOODS?

We all know what dairy foods are, don't we? Maybe not. There is actually quite a lot of confusion about this term. Essentially, it applies to cow's milk, cream, butter, cheese and related items like buttermilk, yogurt, fromage frais and dairy ice cream. Many processed foods contain milk and dairy products. Obvious candidates are milk chocolate and dairy spreads, but there are many other items, too. A detailed list of foods to avoid, plus advice about what to look for on labels, is given elsewhere in this introduction.

ARE WE ONLY SPEAKING ABOUT COW'S MILK?

Technically, yes. Goat's milk and ewe's milk – and their associated products – are not dairy foods, although they have a similar composition to cow's milk, and may cause similar problems for some individuals, although other people will tolerate them quite well.

IS IT OKAY TO GIVE UP MILK?

Before embarking on a dairy-free diet, or even substantially reducing your intake of dairy foods, it is only sensible to seek advice from a doctor or nutritionist. Milk is the most complete food available, providing valuable amounts of protein, fat, carbohydrate (in the form of lactose/milk sugar), vitamin A and – particularly – B2 (riboflavin). It is rich in readily absorbed calcium and also a good source of phosphorus. In young children, who may be picky about what and how much they eat, milk is often the main source of energy. If you give up milk and other dairy products,

AVERAGE CALCIUM VALUES OF DAIRY AND OTHER MILKS

Type of milk	Per 100ml
whole cow's milk (including lactose-reduced)	120mg
semi-skimmed and skimmed cow's milk	120-125mg
evaporated milk	290mg
goat's milk	120mg
sheep's milk	170mg
soya milk	13mg
soya milk (with added calcium)	140mg

Left: Cow's milk dairy products include (clockwise from top left) milk, evaporated milk, fromage frais, condensed milk, dairy spread, curd cheese, butter, buttermilk and cream, and in the centre, cheese and yogurt.

whether in the short term or for longer, it is therefore important to look at other ways of providing these nutrients, especially calcium.

WHY IS CALCIUM SO IMPORTANT?

Calcium is essential for building strong teeth and bones, normal blood clotting, nerve function and enzyme activity. It is particularly important for young children and teenagers, but even after we stop growing, around the age of 18 years, the need for calcium continues. Requirements are also higher during pregnancy and breastfeeding.

Recent research suggests that having adequate amounts of calcium in early life and building up a strong skeletal structure may help to prevent osteoporosis, or "brittle bone disease" in later life. This condition occurs when calcium is lost faster than it can be replaced, and bones become weak and fragile. Taking regular exercise (especially weight-bearing exercise) also helps to strengthen bones. Vitamin D, which is produced by the

Above: Leafy dark green vegetables, such as Savoy cabbage, broccoli, curly kale and spinach, are good sources of calcium.

action of sunlight on the skin, helps with the absorption of calcium by the body, whereas both smoking and excessive drinking of alcohol deplete calcium reserves.

HOW DO WE GET CALCIUM, IF NOT FROM DAIRY FOODS?

There are many other good sources of calcium. These include:

- white or brown bread (fortified)
- leafy dark green vegetables, such as Savoy cabbage, spring greens, curly kale, broccoli and spinach
- canned sardines or pilchards in oil or tomato sauce (provided the bones are eaten)
- canned baked beans in tomato sauce, red kidney beans, chick-peas and lentils
- soya beans and tofu (soya bean curd)
- nuts, particularly almonds, Brazil nuts and hazelnuts
- seeds, such as sesame seeds and sunflower seeds
- dried apricots, dried figs and currants
- muesli

Above: Canned sardines, whether canned in tomato sauce or oil, are a good source of calcium – provided, of course, that you eat the bones along with the fish.

Above: Add extra calcium to your diet by nibbling on dried fruits, such as dried figs and apricots, or add currants to cakes or dried fruit salads.

Above: Soya contains calcium, so it is a good idea to include bean curd (tofu) in your diet – it is delicious added to stir-fries, or use soya beans in casseroles and salads.

WHAT CAUSES A FOOD INTOLERANCE?

Why is it that certain natural foods, which are quite harmless and nutritious in themselves, and which can be happily enjoyed by the majority of people, pose a problem for others? The reasons are not properly understood and there is much research work in progress investigating this complex and often controversial subject. Hopefully we will have more answers in the near future, but in the meantime, suffering from a sensitivity to food can be worrying and distressing for those affected.

Food intolerance is a broad term used to describe many troublesome symptoms associated with food intake, and includes any abnormal reaction that occurs as a result of eating the offending food. An allergy, on the other hand, is a specific extreme reaction, caused by a breakdown in the immune system, which causes the body to react to normally harmless substances.

Many different substances can provoke a reaction, which is why it can sometimes be difficult to pinpoint the offending culprit. Certain foods, including milk and dairy products, eggs, wheat and other cereals, shellfish, nuts (particularly peanuts and peanut products), soya products and citrus fruits are among the most common suspects in cases of food intolerance and allergy. Symptoms may be mild or severe, leading to discomfort, illness or even – in cases of extreme allergic reaction – death. It is therefore vital to isolate which food or foods are causing the problem, so that appropriate action can be taken. Depending upon the severity of the situation, this may mean eating less of the offending food, either temporarily or permanently, or cutting it out altogether.

ARE INTOLERANCES COMMON?

It's hard to say precisely how common food intolerances are, as many cases go undetected. This is particularly true of dairy intolerance, which varies in severity, with many sufferers simply accepting and living with symptoms. However, health visitors and paediatricians are likely to identify feeding problems in babies and infants and will refer patients to a dietician, if necessary. We may also sometimes self-diagnose a suspected intolerance, which is fine if the offending food is something like shellfish or strawberries, which can easily be avoided. But dairy foods are a wide and important group nutritionally so it's wise to seek professional help and advice, especially as some symptoms may have another cause that requires medical treatment.

IS FOOD INTOLERANCE AN INHERITED PROBLEM?

Allergies appear to have a genetic link, so if there's a family history of eczema, asthma or hayfever, children are more likely to suffer a food intolerance problem, particularly if both parents have allergic tendencies.

ARE FOOD INTOLERANCES LESS LIKELY TO OCCUR IF BABIES ARE BREASTFED?

Breastfeeding offers many advantages in terms of convenience and providing perfectly balanced nutrition for a newborn baby. It is often when cow's milk is introduced, either as a modified formula milk or during weaning on to solid foods that unpleasant symptoms related to dairy intolerance may arise. A baby's digestive system is unable to cope with the different composition of cow's milk, so it is recommended that regular unmodified milk should not be introduced before a child is six months old, and ideally not before the first birthday. Some evidence suggests that breastfeeding for at least three months, or better still for four to six months, may offer some protection against cow's milk intolerance. (Gluten, which is the protein in wheat, rye, oats and barley can also cause problems, as can eggs and soya, and should be avoided until after six months of age.)

Above: Fresh eggs, citrus fruits, such as oranges and lemons, peanuts and shellfish, such as prawns, are some of the most common suspects in cases of food sensitivity and allergy.

Above: Grains, such as wheat, rye, oats and barley contain a protein called gluten, which can also cause food intolerance problems and should be avoided in childrens' diets until they are at least six months old.

LACTOSE INTOLERANCE V MILK ALLERGY – WHAT'S THE DIFFERENCE?

LACTOSE INTOLERANCE

This not an allergic reaction but occurs because the body lacks (or does not produce enough of) an enzyme called lactase, which is normally active in the intestinal wall. The function of lactase is to break down lactose (milk sugar) into simpler sugars that can be absorbed by the body. If this doesn't happen, the undigested lactose passes into the large intestine (colon) where it causes irritation and the classic symptoms commonly associated with lactose intolerance. These include bloating, stomach pain, diarrhoea and excessive wind, produced by naturally occurring microflora in the gut, which ferment the undigested lactose and produce gas.

Lactase deficiency is estimated to affect around two-thirds of the world's population. It is more common among non-white/black races, where milk is not a staple food after weaning. However, in Northern Europe, where dairy products are commonly eaten, adults are less likely to have reduced levels of lactase enzyme.

Temporary lactose intolerance can also be triggered by a bout of gastro-enteritis (particularly in young children) or in adults as a consequence of any illness that affects the lining of the small intestine. This sensitivity is generally only short term and usually clears up if the individual avoids cow's milk for a time.

The degree of intolerance varies and may be mild or quite severe. Some people can tolerate small amounts of cow's milk; some find they must avoid drinking milk on its own, but can eat yogurt and some cheeses (which contain little lactose). Some can cope with goat's milk or sheep's milk, although these also contain lactose and can provoke a reaction in susceptible individuals. Other alternative milks, such as soya milk, can also provide suitable substitutes, although for nutritional reasons, establishing an acceptable low level of regular milk is often advised.

MILK ALLERGY

Unlike lactose intolerance, milk allergy is a relatively uncommon condition; and is usually a reaction to the protein (not the lactose) in milk. It is generally restricted to young children, who usually outgrow the problem by the age of two or three. The classic symptoms of an allergy to milk protein are eczema, asthma, allergic rhinitis (a persistent runny nose), vomiting and diarrhoea. In rare instances, the reaction may be severe, and

Right: Milk allergy is relatively uncommon and most young children can drink milk.

Below: Although lactase deficiency can affect people from all nationalities, it is more prevalent in black ethnic groups.

professional guidance should always be sought if an allergy is suspected.

Sometimes, sensitivity to protein and lactose can coexist, particularly after a gastrointestinal upset. The usual treatment is to temporarily exclude milk and dairy products, but again, it is only sensible to seek professional advice from a doctor or nutritionist.

ALLERGIES EXPLAINED

Normally, the immune system acts as a defence mechanism, protecting the body from genuinely harmful substances like bacteria and viruses, thus preventing illnesses. In the allergic or "atopic" person, there's a breakdown in the immune system, causing the body to react to a harmless substance. Allergies do not always occur in isolation. The atopic individual may well be sensitive to several allergens. For instance, someone with a milk allergy may also have a problem with eggs. It is therefore useful to look at the whole subject of allergies in greater depth.

WHAT HAPPENS IN AN ALLERGIC REACTION?

When a susceptible individual encounters an allergen, antibodies called IgE (immunoglobulin E) immediately go into battle. This in turn leads to special "mast" cells in our bodies releasing further chemicals, the best known being histamine, which join the IgE antibodies in attacking the invading material. The result is an allergic reaction, with all its associated symptoms. Depending on where the mast cells are located, for instance in the nose, skin, lungs or intestines, this will be the site of the reaction. Typical allergic reactions and their symptoms include: vomiting and diarrhoea; hayfever; asthma (coughing, wheezing and breathlessness); perennial rhinitis (blocked or runny nose); urticaria or hives (nettle rash); and eczema (mild to severe dry skin condition).

ARE WE BECOMING MORE ALLERGIC?

Allergies (particularly asthma and hay fever) appear to be on the increase and this may be a consequence of twentieth-century living, increased air pollution and more use of chemicals and pesticides. It has also been suggested that because modern medicine has reduced our risk of infection from "naturally" harmful foreign invaders, such as bacteria, our immune systems are not sufficiently challenged to respond to ordinarily harmless substances in genetically susceptible people. Greater awareness and recognition of allergies may also be a factor in our perception of the problem: it is important not to use the term indiscriminately as a convenient scapegoat for all kinds of ailments and complaints that have never been proven to have been caused by an allergic reaction.

WHAT SUBSTANCES ARE PARTICULARLY LIKELY TO BE IMPLICATED?

All kinds of substances, such as pollen, pet hair, dust mites, nickel, insect stings, rubber, make-up, perfume and food can be potential allergens. However, although each allergy exhibits classic symptoms, these symptoms are not exclusive to one type of allergy. It can, therefore, be very difficult to pinpoint precisely which allergen is responsible. For instance, eczema can be related to diet, but dust, pollen, pet hair and various chemicals can also be triggers. Accurate diagnosis and careful monitoring is essential in order to identify the offending culprit(s) before any changes are made to the diet.

All sorts of substances can be potential allergens, from pollen to perfume, and from dust mites to make-up. The symptoms are not exclusive to one type of allergy and the body's reaction can vary from mild to severe. Peanuts and peanut products (left) can cause a severe, and potentially fatal, allergic reaction in some people.

COMMON ALLERGIES AND THEIR SYMPTOMS

Allergic Disease	Allergen	Typical Symptoms
Hayfever (seasonal)	Pollen	Sneezing, streaming eyes, blocked nose
Asthma	Dust mites, animal hair, pollen	Coughing, wheezing, breathlessness
Allergic Rhinitis (perennial)	Dust mites, animal hair	Sneezing, runny nose, itchy eyes
Urticaria (nettle rash)	Food, medicines	Itchy rash, characterized by the eruption of weals or "hives"

FOOD ALLERGIES

Allergic Disease	Allergen	Typical Symptoms
Coeliac Disease	Gluten (protein found in wheat, barley, rye and oats)	Poor growth, weight loss through vomiting and diarrhoea, tiredness
Peanut Allergy	Peanuts (and possibly other nuts and seeds)	Severity varies, but can cause a massive, potentially fatal reaction called anaphylactic shock, where the victim finds it hard to breathe, turns blue around the lips and faints or loses consciousness
Wheat Allergy	Wheat and wheat products	Asthma, itchy skin, diarrhoea
Egg Allergy	Eggs and egg products	Eczema or urticaria
Fish Allergy	Fish and shellfish	Urticaria in mild cases, but can lead to anaphylactic shock in severe cases
Milk Allergy	Milk protein	Eczema, asthma, perennial rhinitis, intestinal upsets

A small minority of people may also be allergic to food additives, both natural and artificial, such as food colours like tartrazine and anatto and preservatives such as benzoate. But as can be clearly seen from the chart, symptoms are often similar for different allergens, so it is essential to pinpoint the true cause or causes.

TRACKING DOWN THE PROBLEM

If you suspect that you or someone in your family may be suffering from an allergy or an intolerance to milk and dairy foods, the first thing to do is make an appointment with your doctor to make sure that your symptoms are not due to any other illness. He or she will try to diagnose the problem by asking questions about your diet and lifestyle and whether you've noticed if symptoms are worse at any particular time. The medical profession varies in its attitude and approach to the treatment of allergies. You may be referred to a special hospital unit or clinic for further investigation or advised to see a dietician, if dietary changes are to be considered. Many clinics offer allergy testing by a variety of methods. While these may prove useful, not all these methods are recognized by the medical profession as providing reliable results.

IS ANY REACTION TO AN ALLERGEN LIKELY TO BE IMMEDIATE?

In cases of severe, acute allergy (which susceptible individuals may experience after eating peanuts, fish, eggs or sesame seeds) reaction is immediate and can be life threatening. After a first attack, those affected will be well aware of their allergy. It is vital that they avoid the offending food and always carry appropriate treatment, such as steroid inhalers, antihistamine tablets or emergency adrenaline (for anaphylaxis/ anaphylactic shock).

Acute reactions to milk (and wheat) tend to be less severe and are often delayed (12–48 hours after ingesting the trigger food). In infants, severe acute reaction can occur, but as the diet is limited, the offending trigger is usually obvious – as when formula milk is introduced after breastfeeding. Recurring headaches, skin complaints, sinus or digestive problems are likely to be caused by something environmental or something eaten regularly, which is why dairy or wheat is often suspected.

WHAT METHODS ARE USED TO TEST FOR ALLERGIES OR INTOLERANCES?

The RAST (Radio Allergo Sorbent Test): This test can sometimes be used for identifying acute allergies when there's an immediate reaction, by measuring IgE antibody levels in the blood.

The Skin Prick Test: A few drops of the suspect allergen (prepared to a standardized concentration) are put on the skin, which is then pricked, so that the allergen seeps underneath. After a brief delay, the allergist looks for signs of a reaction. This test is quite successful for detecting environmental allergies, such as pollens or cat hair, which exhibit immediate sensitivity, but may be less useful for food intolerances which are often delayed.

The Vega Test: In this test, an electrode is placed on an acupuncture point or held in the hand. It is said to detect whether a substance placed on the machine causes you to react, but again tests may not be reliable.

Lactose intolerance in infants may be diagnosed by checking stools for acidity (lactic acid is a by-product of the fermentation of undigested lactose).

Exclusion and Challenge Diets: These provide the most accurate and effective means of discovering a food intolerance. They work very simply: the sufferer excludes suspect foods, waits to see whether there is an improvement in symptoms, then gradually reintroduces them to see if the symptoms return.

Left: If you suspect that you or someone in your family may be suffering from an allergy, the first thing to do is make an appointment with your doctor who will try to diagnose the problem.

SOLVING THE PROBLEM

THE DAIRY-FREE DIET

It must be stressed that it is not advisable to embark on a strict exclusion diet without medical supervision or without the help of a state-registered dietician who will be able to advise on whether replacement foods are advisable and who may recommend supplements to ensure balanced nutrition.

I'VE BEEN ADVISED TO TRY AN EXCLUSION DIET. WHAT HAPPENS NOW?

An exclusion diet must be followed for at least two weeks to see if there is any noticeable improvement. You'll need to stick to it faithfully and keep a food diary to record your results.

Below: If you are tackling an exclusion diet, you'll need to keep a note of the foods that you eat each day and record the results in a notebook or diary.

There are various different ways of tackling an exclusion diet, and the one you follow will depend whether you already know what the trigger foods are (in this case dairy foods); whether you simply suspect that some or all dairy products may be implicated; or whether there's a chance there may be other problem foods.

TRY IT AND SEE

This simple approach involves cutting down on dairy foods to see if there's any improvement. This may be effective if the problem is caused by a lactose intolerance (as often small amounts of lactose can be tolerated), but symptoms may continue if there's a more acute intolerance or allergy.

SIMPLE EXCLUSION DIET

Try totally excluding all milk and dairy products for two to four weeks, then assess if there's any improvement. A list of foods to avoid appears elsewhere in this introduction.

AVOIDING COMMON TRIGGERS

This may be suggested if the offending food is not known. You'll be advised to cut out the common suspects like dairy products, wheat, corn, soya, citrus fruits, eggs, nuts, chocolate, tea, coffee and additives and will then be asked to reintroduce one food at a time, keeping track of any reaction.

FEW FOODS (ELIMINATION) DIET (STRICT)

This is only to be used in severe cases where a condition such as eczema responds poorly to prescribed skin treatment. It involves going on a very basic diet of only five to seven fresh foods (lamb, potatoes, rice, pears, cauliflower/broccoli, sunflower or olive oil and bottled water), which are thought least likely to cause an allergic response. Other foods are then gradually reintroduced so that the offending foods can be identified when symptoms recur. This diet is very restrictive and requires careful medical supervision, but can be useful if multiple intolerances are suspected.

When adhering to any exclusion diet, remember that factors other than food may influence the results. You'll need to be patient, as there may be several triggers causing the problem.

The good news is that excluding milk and its products needn't be daunting or difficult – the recipes in this book will give you lots of delicious dairy-free ideas for providing varied and nourishing menus.

Children usually outgrow food allergies and should not stay on a milk-free diet for longer than necessary.

Note: If your doctor has prescribed medication for treatment of asthma or eczema, such as inhalers, emollients or steroid creams, these shouldn't be stopped but used in conjunction with dietary treatment.

FOODS THAT ARE SAFE TO EAT

Recipes and ingredients will vary between different manufacturers, so it is impossible to give a definitive safe list, but there are certain generic food categories that do not contain dairy products. These include:

- fruit (fresh, canned, frozen)
- fruit juices (fresh, frozen, canned, bottled and UHT)
- fish (fresh, frozen without batter, crumb coating or sauce, canned)
- meat, poultry, game, bacon, offal and Quorn (not processed products)
- pasta (fresh and dried), rice and other grains
- beans and pulses (dried and canned)
- nuts and seeds
- vegetables (fresh, frozen, dried)

In addition, the following items can generally be eaten safely, but always check the labels:

BAKING INGREDIENTS
- flour, cornflour, arrowroot
- high quality dark chocolate

- mincemeat
- marzipan, ready-to-roll icing
- desiccated coconut, creamed coconut
- dried fruit, glacé cherries, candied peel, canned fruit pie fillings
- ready-to-use pastry is safe if made with pure vegetable fat
- filo (brush with oil, not melted butter, when layering)

BEVERAGES
- fresh fruit juices and soft drinks
- beef, yeast or vegetable extract drinks
- most types of drinking chocolate powder and cocoa powder

BISCUITS
- grissini (breadsticks), cream crackers, water biscuits
- oatcakes, crispbreads, rice cakes, melba toast and matzos are usually dairy-free

BREADS AND BAKED GOODS
- bagels, pitta breads and muffins are usually dairy-free

- some ready made pizza bases are dairy-free

CAKES AND PASTRIES
- meringues
- some fruit pies are dairy-free

CEREALS
- most breakfast cereals, such as Cornflakes, Shreddies, Weetabix
- porridge oats and some brands of muesli
- couscous, bulgur wheat, semolina

CONFECTIONERY AND SNACK FOODS
- mints, jellies, pastilles, marshmallows, some plain chocolate, carob
- all kinds of nuts, tortilla chips, taco shells, pretzels, poppadums, prawn crackers and some crisps

DAIRY MILK SUBSTITUTES
- soya "milk" drinks
- nut "milks", rice drinks
- goat's or sheep's milk (if tolerated)
- lactose-reduced milk (if tolerated)

Above: Many baking ingredients are dairy-free. Clockwise from top left, yellow and white marzipan, plain dark cooking chocolate, canned fruit pie filling, desiccated coconut, glacé cherries and cornflour

Above: Some people can tolerate goat's milk, sheep's milk and lactose-reduced milk.

DELI FOODS
- cooked, sliced meats
- some ready-made salads, such as mixed bean salad, Waldorf salad, carrot and nut salad
- Florida salad, potato salad, coleslaw in mayonnaise, but check that yogurt has not been used in place of the mayonnaise

DESSERTS
- jellies
- custard powder (not the instant type)
- sorbets and pure fruit ice lollies
- soya desserts and soya yogurts
- goat's and sheep's milk yogurts (these are not lactose-free, so eat with caution)

DIPS
- taramasalata, hummus and fresh tomato or fruit salsas

FATS AND OILS
- pure solid vegetable oil, soya spread/margarine, kosher margarine, lard, beef and vegetable suet
- corn, sunflower, safflower, olive, soya, rapeseed and nut oils
- mayonnaise, salad cream, Thousand Island dressing (without yogurt) and French dressing

FISH AND FISH PRODUCTS
- canned fish or shellfish in brine or oil
- smoked fish

MEAT PRODUCTS
- most sausages and burgers are dairy-free, but check ingredients

MISCELLANEOUS
- bouillon cubes
- gravy powders and granules
- herbs and spices
- olives
- onion bhajis
- pakoras
- samosas
- stuffings and breadcrumbs
- vegetable spring rolls
- vinegar

Above: Many ready-made deli salsas and salads are dairy-free – and perfect to eat with pitta bread. Try taramasalata, tomato salsa, carrot and nut salad and coleslaw.

Right: Finding the right dairy-free snack shouldn't be too troublesome – you can safely eat tortilla chips, poppadums, some crisps, prawn crackers and taco shells.

SAUCES AND CONDIMENTS
- relishes, chutneys, pickles
- soy sauce
- mustard
- tomato ketchup, tomato purée, sun-dried tomato paste
- most tomato-based pasta sauces

SOUPS
- French onion, spring vegetable, oxtail, lentil, consommé and minestrone should be safe but many creamed varieties include dairy products

SOYA PRODUCTS
- soya mince/chunks
- tofu (soya bean curd)
- soya cheese/spreads

SWEET AND SAVOURY SPREADS
- jams and marmalades, honey
- peanut butter
- sandwich spreads and pastes (check ingredients)

VEGETARIAN PRODUCTS
- most burgers, rissoles and sausages are dairy-free, as are all vegan products

Some "ready meals" (chilled and frozen) are dairy-free. Check the label on individual packages.

FOODS TO AVOID

As well as all the familiar dairy foods, many dairy products and derivatives are used in a wide range of processed foods. Depending on how strict your dairy-free diet needs to be, it may be necessary to avoid all of these foods or just some of them. Check labels if unsure of the ingredients, as there will be variation between products and brands, and take advice from a dietician.

COMMON DAIRY FOODS
- milk (skimmed, semi-skimmed, whole and powdered)
- evaporated and condensed milk
- cream
- crème fraîche
- fromage frais
- Quark
- butter
- buttermilk
- cheese
- yogurt

PROCESSED FOODS THAT MAY CONTAIN DAIRY INGREDIENTS

BEVERAGES AND DRINKS
- coffee whitener
- malted milk drinks
- instant hot chocolate drinks (powdered drinking chocolate and cocoa are usually dairy free)
- milkshakes

BISCUITS
- most sweet types and some flavoured (for instance, with cheese) savoury varieties
- some cereal bars (check label)

BREAD AND BAKED GOODS
- many contain dairy products (check ingredients on individual items)

BREAKFAST CEREALS
- some muesli-type and some oaty cereals contain skimmed milk powder.

CAKES
- many contain dairy products

CONFECTIONERY
- milk and some plain chocolate
- fudge
- toffee

DESSERTS
- custards (ready-made canned, fresh chilled and instant custard mix)
- ready-made dairy-type desserts and mousses (fresh, chilled and frozen)
- cheesecakes
- ice cream (dairy and non-dairy – usually made from skimmed milk and vegetable fat)
- pancakes and batter mixes
- canned rice puddings and other dairy puddings
- pudding mixes

Right: There are many processed foods that may contain dairy products, from fairly obvious cream cakes, milk chocolates and cream toffees to less easy to spot muesli, savoury biscuits and other baked goods.

Left: Dairy ice cream and milk chocolate are two dairy foods that unfortunately have to be avoided. Even non-dairy ice cream may have skimmed milk power or other dairy products added, so always check the ingredients label.

- frankfurters and some sausages
- some sausage rolls, pies and pastries
- pizzas (some pizza bases are dairy-free to use with your own topping)
- some savoury pie fillings
- creamy sauces
- many fresh, canned and dried soups
- quiches and flans
- dips based on yogurt, fromage frais or cheese

FATS AND SPREADS
- dairy spreads
- margarine (most brands contain some buttermilk, skimmed milk or whey powder)
- low or reduced-fat spreads (may contain buttermilk)

SAVOURY FOODS
- some breadcrumbed and battered items
- Yorkshire puddings
- some "ready meals" (fresh, chilled and frozen)

SWEET PRESERVES AND SPREADS
- chocolate spread/chocolate and hazelnut spread
- luxury lemon curd

VEGETABLES, CANNED OR PACKAGED
- creamed corn
- creamed mushrooms
- instant mashed potato
- spaghetti (canned in tomato sauce)

ALWAYS REMEMBER TO CHECK THE INGREDIENT LABELS ON PACKAGED FOODS

This list can only serve as a guide as recipes vary between products and manufacturers. This is especially true of processed foods. If one brand is off limits because it contains dairy foods, check all similar products; the next one along on the shelf may be dairy-free. It is also important to check items bought from pharmacies: some sweeteners, medicines and vitamin tablets/capsules may contain dairy ingredients, such as lactose.

Below left: Dairy spreads, most margarines, some brands of lemon curd, and chocolate spread all contain dairy products.

Below right: Avoid canned and packaged vegetables, such as creamed sweetcorn and mushrooms, canned spaghetti in tomato sauce and instant mashed potato – they all contain dairy products.

SUBSTITUTE FOODS

There's no need to miss out on choice or taste on a dairy-free diet. A wide range of alternative products is available in supermarkets, health food shops and wholefood stores as well as from specialist mail-order companies. These substitutes can be used to replace regular cow's milk in hot and cold drinks, on breakfast cereals and for all your favourite recipes. If you can tolerate goat's or sheep's milk, these are also available from large supermarkets and health food shops, or you may well find a local farm or farm shop with supplies of milk, yogurt and cheese. Milks and creams can be frozen successfully for 2-3 months, which is a real bonus if your supplier lives some distance away.

ALTERNATIVES TO COW'S MILK

GOAT'S AND SHEEP'S MILK
Both goat's and sheep's milk are just as versatile as cow's milk. Goat's milk has a stronger, tangier taste than cow's milk. Sheep's milk has a higher fat content so is thicker and tastes richer and creamier. It is also slightly sweet, so it is ideal for use in milk puddings. Some individuals who have an intolerance to cow's milk find that they react quite well to these alternatives, but it must be stressed that both goat's milk and sheep's milk can provoke an allergic reaction. Their protein content is similar, although not the same as cow's milk. Neither goat's milk nor sheep's milk is lactose-free, so they may well be unsuitable for anyone with more than a mild intolerance. The only way to find out if they are acceptable is to try them and see. (These milks are not recommended for infants under one year of age.)

Goat's cream is available from some larger supermarkets and health food shops. It has a smooth, sweet taste and can be used as a pouring cream, or whipped and used in desserts and as a topping or filling for cakes.

SOYA "MILKS"/DRINKS
These drinks are made from soya beans and are widely available, fresh chilled and in UHT cartons, in unsweetened and sweetened versions and as flavoured varieties. They are often fortified with calcium, as soya milk is naturally low in calcium compared with cow's milk, and may also have added vitamins. Soya drinks are lactose free, low in fat (also some fat-free and full-fat versions are available) and free of cholesterol and may therefore offer positive health benefits. In countries where soya foods are eaten regularly there appears to be less risk of developing certain cancers. The incidence of coronary heart disease and menopausal symptoms also appear to be reduced.

Plain soya milk can be used as a complete milk replacement in hot and cold beverages and for all kinds of recipes. The flavoured varieties, such as vanilla and chocolate, make an appetizing "milky" drink.

However, some allergic individuals may react to the soya protein and – as with goat's and sheep's milk – soya milk is not recommended for infants under the age of 12 months. Where a baby reacts to regular formula milks, dieticians generally advise changing to a special non-allergenic modified formula milk.

Soya "cream" is a non-dairy alternative to single cream and is widely available in long-life cartons from health food shops and supermarkets.

Left: Alternative milk drinks include (clockwise from top left) sheep's milk, lactose-reduced milk, soya milk, goat's milk, soya cream, oat drink and rice drink.

OAT DRINK

This is a Swedish product made with whole oats, rapeseed oil and pure spring water. It is low in fat and calories, contains no cholesterol and offers another alternative for those on a dairy-free diet. UHT cartons are available from health food shops.

RICE DRINK

Another long-life drink, this is made from filtered water, organic rice syrup, sunflower oil, sea salt and vanilla flavouring. It is lactose-free and low in fat and is suitable for vegans or those with a milk allergy or intolerance.

FORMS OF COW'S MILK THAT MAY BE TOLERATED

LACTOSE-REDUCED MILK

This is a long-life, full cream product. Although it is made from cow's milk, its lactose content has been reduced through the addition of a natural lactase enzyme, similar to that normally found in the digestive system.

HEAT-TREATED MILKS

Certain milk proteins are affected by heat treatment, which alters their composition and makes them tolerable for older children and adults. You may therefore find that sterilized, UHT and evaporated milk are acceptable if an intolerance is caused by protein rather than lactose.

YOGURTS AND DESSERTS

Yogurt is a fermented milk product, which may contain bacteria with enzymes that can digest the lactose present in the milk to produce lactic acid. It is therefore low in lactose, so even yogurt derived from cow's milk may be acceptable for people with relatively mild lactose intolerance. If cow's milk doesn't suit you but you can tolerate goat's or sheep's milk, you'll find a ready supply of these yogurts. There is also a good range of soya desserts, yogurts and ice cream.

CHEESES

Hard cheeses like Cheddar, Stilton and Parmesan are relatively low in lactose so small amounts may be safe to eat without causing symptoms.

Alternatively, vegan cheeses, made from soya protein, are available from wholefood or health food shops. There are several types, including variations on Cheddar, Gouda, Stilton, Edam, Parmesan and mozzarella. These cheeses can be used in sandwiches or in cooking, although they may not melt in exactly the same way as similar dairy cheeses.

There's also a good selection of goat's and sheep's cheeses available. Goat's cheeses include Chabichou, Chevrotin, Crottin de Chavignol, Chèvre and Chèvre Roulé, Capricorn and Mendip.

Sheep's (ewe's) milk cheeses include Roquefort and pecorino, and also feta and haloumi. These cheeses are traditionally made from sheep's milk but some brands may be made from or contain some cow's milk, so, as with all food products, it is important to check the label.

Above: The huge range of dairy-free soya products available include (clockwise from top left) soya yogurt, soya dessert, soya milk, marinated tofu, smoked tofu, hard cheeses, which are similar to Cheddar, Edam and mozzarella, "cream" cheese and (centre) silken tofu.

FATS AND SPREADS

Choose from "dairy-free" soya spreads, vegetarian or kosher margarines or pure vegetable fats and oils. These can all be used for spreading, baking, sauces and stir-frying. Check labels on vegetable margarines as they often contain some whey or buttermilk, which is added to bring out the flavour, but is obviously unacceptable to anyone on a dairy-free diet.

TOFU (SOYA BEAN CURD)

This is a high-protein, low-fat food made from soya beans. It comes in a block with a firm or soft (silken) texture and is available plain, marinated or smoked. Tofu in all its forms is very versatile and can be used in a wide variety of ways as a basis for both sweet and savoury dishes.

READ THE LABELS

If you are following a dairy-free diet – or even just cutting down on your consumption of dairy foods, it is vital that you read the labels of cans and packages before buying any processed or ready-made foods. By law, food labels must list all the ingredients in order of weight and the lists may be quite lengthy. It may seem to be rather time-consuming scrutinizing labels to begin with, but you'll soon get to know which foods are safe for you to eat, and which you should avoid.

WHAT IF THERE IS NO LIST OF INGREDIENTS?

There is no legal requirement to list ingredients on products sold loose and unpackaged on the delicatessen counter, butcher and bakery counters where it would be difficult to include such information on the display ticket. If you need to know more about a product, ask the sales assistant or department manager, who should have

access to a product information guide and who will be able to advise you.

CAN I EXPECT ADVICE FROM MY SUPERMARKET?

All major supermarkets will provide detailed lists of all their milk-free products (as well as "free from" lists for eggs, gluten, wheat, additives, soya and peanuts and foods that are suitable for vegetarians and vegans). Simply ask at the Customer Information desk for the number to call. Many supermarkets also have a Customer Care Line you can phone for detailed information about products. Check the product packaging, too – it may well list the manufacturer's own helpline number.

EASIER LABELLING

To make it easier to spot allergens in ingredients lists, many manufacturers

have recently added an additional information box underneath the ingredients list, highlighting the presence of any of the major problem foods. This box states "★contains" followed by the name of the food, such as milk, eggs or nuts.

PRODUCT CHANGES AND VARIATIONS

From time to time, manufacturers may change the formulation of their products, perhaps to improve a recipe or because they change their supplier, so don't assume a product is safe to eat simply because you've bought it before. Always check the label.

Below: Make sure that you check the label of processed foods – those on cans, bottles and packaged foods must by law list the ingredients in order of weight.

OTHER NAMES FOR MILK AND MILK PRODUCTS

Milk and milk products often crop up in the most unlikely places and with names the uninitiated might fail to recognize, so look out for the following ingredients, which are all names for different forms of milk and its derivatives.

casein	skimmed milk whey
caseinates	
ghee	skimmed milk powder
hydrolyzed casein	hydrolyzed milk protein
lactose	whey
lactalbumin	whey protein
milk sugar	whey sugar
milk solids	whey syrup sweetener
non-fat milk solids	

HOW TO ADAPT YOUR DIET

If you are considering switching to a dairy-free diet, or have done so only recently, like any change in lifestyle it will take a little getting used to. However, with the wide range of foods available in supermarkets and the ever-increasing selection of dairy-alternative products, you'll be surprised at how quickly you can adjust your food choices and eating habits. Aim to eat a good, balanced diet, with plenty of fresh fruit and vegetables, high-fibre (particularly wholewheat) starchy carbohydrates, such as rice, pasta and potatoes, and only moderate amounts of foods that are high in fat – particularly animal fats – and sugar. For a good intake of calcium, choose leafy green vegetables, such as cabbage and broccoli, canned sardines, bread, pulses, cereals, dried fruits, seeds and nuts.

DAIRY-FREE SHOPPING

It's amazing what you can find in the supermarket when you actively start looking for it. Although there is an enormous range of familiar dairy products, non-dairy items are also well represented. Thanks to the multi-cultural nature of our society, a far greater variety of foreign and ethnic foods continue to be introduced into supermarkets for all of us to enjoy.

DAIRY-FREE COOKING

Dairy substitutes, such as soya milk, can be used as a straight swap for milk, for pouring over cereals, in hot and cold drinks or for sweet and savoury recipes. If you don't like the taste of one milk, try another brand, as they vary considerably. In cooking, milk substitutes can be used for milk puddings, pancakes, sweet and savoury sauces and soups. They can also be used when baking breads, cakes and biscuits. Vegetables don't have to be served with melted butter; sprinkle them lightly with olive oil instead. For further inspiration, look no further than the recipes in this book – they will provide lots more delicious ideas for family meals and for entertaining.

Above right: Dairy-free desserts include (clockwise from top left) strawberry- and chocolate-flavoured soya desserts, soya yogurt, and sheep's and goat's milk yogurt if these can be tolerated.

Below: Start the day with fruit juice, wholewheat cereal and wholewheat toast.

SAMPLE MENU FOR A DAIRY-FREE DAY

BREAKFAST
Fruit juice
Wholewheat cereal with dairy-
   free milk
Thick slice of wholemeal toast
   spread with soya margarine
   and or jam/marmalade, honey
   or yeast extract

LUNCH
Seafood risotto or
Olive and oregano bread with
   hummus and salad
Figs and pears in honey or
   chilled soya dessert

DINNER
Pork in sweet-and-sour sauce,
   served with rice or noodles
Large portion of spinach, broccoli
   or spring greens
Fresh fruit salad or
   baked apple stuffed with nuts,
   dried fruit and syrup

EATING OUT

When following any restrictive diet, the best option is usually to go for plain, simply cooked foods where you can be fairly sure of the ingredients used. Any dish that uses a combination of ingredients could be suspect. It is always worth asking the chef for further information about a recipe, but if the restaurant is busy, this may not always be convenient. If possible, ask to see the menu in advance, then discuss with the chef any queries you have or special requests. Most restaurants are only too happy to help with special diets, given fair warning and consideration.

LUNCH AND DINNER INVITATIONS

If invited to a friend's or work colleague's home for a meal, do let your host know beforehand that you are following a dairy-free diet (or any special diet), so that he or she can cater accordingly. This prevents any awkwardness or embarrassment, and during the conversation you can discuss how your needs can be accommodated without too much difficulty or inconvenience. It may even be a nice gesture to offer to contribute to the meal by bringing a dessert, which you and others can share and enjoy.

GENERAL GUIDELINES
- avoid anything cooked with cream or butter
- pastries, cakes and puddings may be made with dairy products, so always check first
- many desserts are made with butter, cream and milk. Eggs are also frequently used, which may also be a problem food for those with a dairy intolerance

WHICH NATION'S CUISINE CATERS BEST FOR DAIRY-FREE DIETS?

Chinese cooking uses little dairy produce, relying heavily on rice and noodles, vegetables, fish, tofu and soya bean sauces, making it an excellent option. Vegetable or nut oils are used with exotic spices for flavouring.

Italian food is famous for pizzas, pastas and risottos. Some of these may be suitable, depending on the recipe. Butter is widely used in the cooking of northern Italy, whereas olive oil is favoured in the south. Parmesan and mozzarella cheeses are widely used (and can be tolerated by some people with dairy intolerance) but you can always opt for a pasta dish with a rich tomato sauce or choose your own cheeseless pizza topping with chunky vegetables, olives, spicy meats, seafood and anchovies. Fresh fish and salads are also a good choice. Olive oil is also good for making breads, with fragrant fresh herbs and garlic for flavouring.

Indian restaurants offer a delicious selection of curries and tasty vegetable and pulse dishes. Traditionally, ghee (clarified butter) is used for cooking but nowadays vegetable ghee or vegetable oil is generally used. Some dishes include yogurt. You'll need to avoid anything creamy like korma or pasanda curry but ask for advice. Dairy products feature largely in Indian desserts but there's always a fresh fruit or sorbet option.

French food tends to use a lot of dairy products and many recipes are rich in butter, cream and cheese. Go for simple choices.

Mediterranean and Chinese cuisines offer plenty of dairy-free choices. Try pasta tossed with tomatoes and olives (left), or stir-fried Duck with Pineapple (below).

SOME DAIRY-FREE MENUS

CHINESE-STYLE
Crispy aromatic duck with
    mandarin pancakes
Lemon chicken
Vegetable chow mein
Fried rice or noodles
Fresh lychees with ginger syrup

INDIAN-STYLE
Seekh or shami kebab with salad
Meat, poultry, prawn or
    vegetable curry (avoid curries
    made with yogurt or cream)
Pilau rice
Poppadums
Mango sorbet

SPANISH-STYLE
Melon
Seafood paella
Green salad
Pears baked in red wine

ITALIAN-STYLE
Antipasti of cold meats, sardines,
    tuna, beans and salad
Pasta with sun-dried tomato sauce
Focaccia
Fresh peaches with strawberries

MIDDLE-EASTERN-STYLE
Taramasalata and hummus with
    pitta bread
Lamb tagine with dried fruits
    and honey
Bulgur wheat with toasted nuts
Fresh orange salad
Stuffed dates and Turkish delight

PUB MENU
Tomato salad or
    avocado vinaigrette
Grilled fish or steak or
    lamb cutlets
French fries
Petit pois and grilled tomatoes
Summer pudding or fresh fruit
    salad (no cream)

*Chocolate mousse (above) looks tempting,
but may contain cream as well as milk
chocolate; soup (left) may contain hidden
cream; and moussaka (below left) may
include lots of cheese — all are best avoided.*

DAIRY DISHES TO AVOID

STARTERS
Creamed soups, cheese tart, garlic
bread, guacamole, mousses, pâtés

MAIN COURSES
Creamy sauces, chicken Kiev, fish
pie/fish cakes, gratin Dauphinoise,
lasagne, moussaka, pasta carbonara

PUDDINGS/DESSERTS
Bread and butter pudding,
chocolate desserts, cheesecakes,
crème caramel, crème brûlée, ice
creams, profiteroles, tiramisu/trifle

GREAT CHOICES FOR CHILDREN

All children need a healthy diet for energy, growth and physical and mental development. And, if you establish good eating habits while a child is young, this will encourage healthy eating and sensible food choices throughout life.

Since cow's milk provides the major source of protein, energy, calcium, Vitamin A and Vitamin B2 (riboflavin) in the diet of a young child, it is vital to give complete nutritional substitutes if dairy foods aren't eaten. Taking a child off any important group of foods is quite safe provided you replace them with foods that have equal nutritional value – and which will be eaten with relish, such as calcium-enriched dairy-free soya products.

Children don't like to be different from their peers, so don't make an issue about any special dietary requirements. Just help your child to understand why certain foods may not be allowed and which food choices to make. Unfortunately, being told that a certain food should be avoided or restricted doesn't stop us craving it – dairy foods like custard, rice pudding, chocolate and ice cream rank among children's favourites, so it is very important to find acceptable substitutes. The good news is that although milk allergies are more common amongst infants and pre-school children, they are generally short-lived, so your child may well outgrow an intolerance.

DON'T LET YOUR CHILD MISS BREAKFAST

Breakfast is the most important meal of the day. It kick-starts the body first thing in the morning and provides energy and nutrients to keep us fit and alert through the morning. Children who skip breakfast can be lethargic and lack concentration, so make sure there's enough time for them to eat something nourishing, even if it means getting up ten minutes earlier. Breakfast can be boring if it is always the same, so shop for a variety of different cereals and baked goods like bagels or muffins (many are dairy-free) and stock up with a choice of fresh and canned fruits, soya yogurts and alternative "milk" drinks.

SOME BREAKFAST IDEAS
- hash browns with poached egg and grilled bacon
- English muffin spread with peanut butter and topped with sliced banana
- flavoured soya drink or milkshake/ smoothie made with soya "milk"
- baked beans on toast (check that the bread is milk-free)
- scrambled eggs made without milk and cooked in pure vegetable margarine, served with grilled tomatoes (and sausage)
- fresh fruit salad or dried fruit compote, cooked in apple juice
- cereal bar (check ingredients) plus an apple or pear

SCHOOL DINNERS
There are almost always two or three choices on a school dinner menu (although favourite dishes tend to go first, so last in the queue have a limited selection), so there should always be something suitable for a dairy-free diet. School caterers are generally keen to provide a helpful service and will meet with parents (and a dietician if

Left: Most children enjoy cooking and preparing foods, so let them help out in the kitchen – as a bonus, they'll find out about the ingredients in different dishes, too.

suggested) to discuss any individual dietary requirements. Always make sure the school knows about any special diet, then arrange an appointment with the catering company or canteen supervisor who will be able to help and advise on specific recipe ingredients and alternative options.

SOME LUNCHTIME IDEAS

Some of the items listed, particularly the puddings and cakes, may have a dairy element, so always ask.

- beef or vegetable burger in a bun with ketchup and salad
- roast chicken with roast potatoes and vegetables
- chicken curry with rice
- spaghetti with meatballs
- sausage casserole
- jacket potato without butter, topped with tuna or baked beans
- lamb and potato hot-pot
- sweet-and-sour chicken served with sweetcorn and rice

FOR DESSERT
- fruit crumble
- lemon meringue pie
- treacle tart
- jam sponge
- flapjack or cherry cake
- fruit jelly

PACKED LUNCHES

Many schools no longer provide a hot school dinner, or your child may prefer a lunch box. This may also be the easier option as you can be certain the contents are safe for your child to eat. Just impress upon him or her that swapping with friends is not an option! Make the lunch fun and varied, pack it in a rigid, insulated cool box and include an ice pack if any of the items are perishable.

A WELL-BALANCED LUNCH WOULD BE:
- a baguette or pitta bread stuffed with tuna and salad

Above: Spaghetti with meatballs is a popular dairy-free choice for children, while fruit crumble made with pure vegetable margarine, or rice pudding made with dairy-free milk (right) would be delicious for dessert.

- fresh fruit or vegetable, such as an apple or a carrot
- calcium-enriched dairy-free pudding, such as a soya dessert. Alternatively, if your child can tolerate it, a regular yogurt
- fun choice, such as a dairy-free cake or a packet of nuts and raisins
- dairy-free drink

HIGH TEAS AND EVENING MEALS

Make all the children's favourite dishes like macaroni cheese, quiche, pancakes, custards and milk puddings by simply substituting alternative milks.

- make a quick, safe pasta carbonara, using soya cheese with garlic and herbs mixed with soya milk, bacon, eggs and peas
- stock up the fridge and freezer with soya desserts and soya ice creams – they make yummy puddings
- dairy-free ice creams can be used to make delicious sundaes, piled high with jelly and fresh fruits
- prepare and freeze fresh fruit purées to pour over desserts
- use pure vegetable fat or oils for making home-made cakes, pastries, biscuits and puddings

CHOCOLATE

Several mail-order companies supply chocolates made without dairy milk, including dairy-free Easter eggs and bunnies and Christmas novelties, so no child need ever miss out on treats.

SOUPS AND STARTERS

When you can start your meal with delicious Chilled Almond Soup

or the more unusual Hot-and-sour Soup, who needs cream? If you do

crave something velvety, however, just dip your spoon into Winter

Vegetable Soup – both the texture and the flavour are sensational.

As for starters, could anything be more colourful and tasty than

Marinated Vegetable Antipasto, Pepper Gratin or the taste sensation

that is Tuna Carpaccio?

Chilled Almond Soup

Use a food processor to prepare this creamy Spanish soup, which is very simple to make and refreshing on a hot day.

INGREDIENTS

Serves 6

115g/4oz fresh white bread
115g/4oz/1 cup blanched almonds
2 garlic cloves, sliced
75ml/5 tbsp olive oil
25ml/1½ tbsp sherry vinegar
salt and freshly ground black pepper
toasted flaked almonds and seedless
 green and black grapes, halved and
 skinned, to garnish

1 Break the bread into a bowl and pour over 150ml/¼ pint/⅔ cup cold water. Leave for 5 minutes.

2 Put the almonds and garlic in a blender or food processor and process until very finely ground. Blend in the soaked white bread.

3 Gradually add the oil until the mixture forms a smooth paste. Add the sherry vinegar, then 600ml/ 1 pint/2½ cups cold water and process until smooth.

4 Transfer to a bowl and season with salt and pepper, adding a little more water if the soup is very thick. Chill for at least 2–3 hours.

5 Ladle the soup into bowls and scatter with the toasted almonds and skinned grapes.

NUTRITION NOTES	
Per portion:	
Energy	251kcals/1044kJ
Protein	5.8g
Fat	20.4g
Saturated Fat	2.3g
Carbohydrate	11.7g
Fibre	1.8g
Sugars	2g
Calcium	68mg

Winter Vegetable Soup

Parsnips, pumpkin and carrots give this soup a wonderfully rich texture and a vibrant colour.

INGREDIENTS

Serves 4
15ml/1 tbsp olive or sunflower oil
15g/½oz/1 tbsp soya margarine
1 onion, chopped
225g/8oz carrots, chopped
225g/8oz parsnips, chopped
225g/8oz pumpkin
about 900ml/1½ pints/3¾ cups
   vegetable or chicken stock
lemon juice, to taste
salt and freshly ground black pepper

For the garnish
7.5ml/1½ tsp olive oil
½ garlic clove, finely chopped
45ml/3 tbsp chopped fresh parsley and
   coriander, mixed
good pinch of paprika

4 To make the garnish, heat the oil in a small pan and gently fry the garlic and herbs for 1–2 minutes. Add the paprika and stir well.

5 Adjust the seasoning of the soup and stir in lemon juice to taste. Pour into warmed individual soup bowls and spoon a little garnish on top, which should then be carefully swirled into the soup.

--- NUTRITION NOTES ---

Per portion:

Energy	139kcals/579kJ
Protein	3.8g
Fat	8.4g
Saturated Fat	2.9g
Carbohydrate	12.7g
Fibre	5.5g
Sugars	7.8g
Calcium	103mg

1 Heat the oil and margarine in a large pan and fry the onion for about 3 minutes until softened, stirring occasionally. Add the carrots and parsnips, stir well, cover and cook over a gentle heat for a further 5 minutes.

2 Cut the pumpkin into chunks, discarding the skin and pith, and stir into the pan. Cover and cook for a further 5 minutes, then add the stock and seasoning and slowly bring to the boil. Cover and simmer very gently for 35–40 minutes until the vegetables are tender.

3 Allow the soup to cool slightly, then purée in a food processor or blender until smooth, adding a little extra water if necessary. Pour back into a clean pan and reheat gently.

Chicken Soup with Vermicelli

This lightly spiced, nourishing soup is chunky enough to serve as a main course. For more than 6 servings, use a whole chicken.

INGREDIENTS

Serves 4
30ml/2 tbsp sunflower oil
15g/½oz/1 tbsp soya margarine
1 onion, chopped
2 chicken legs or breast
   pieces, halved
seasoned flour, for dusting
2 carrots, cut into 4cm/1½in pieces
1 parsnip, cut into 4cm/1½in pieces
1.5 litres/2½ pints/6¼ cups chicken
   stock
1 cinnamon stick
good pinch of paprika
pinch of saffron
2 egg yolks
juice of ½ lemon
30ml/2 tbsp chopped fresh coriander
30ml/2 tbsp chopped fresh parsley
150g/5oz vermicelli
salt and freshly ground black pepper
crusty bread, to serve

1 Heat the oil and soya margarine in a saucepan or flameproof casserole and fry the onion for 3–4 minutes until softened. Dust the chicken pieces in flour and fry gently.

2 Transfer the chicken to a plate and add the carrots and parsnip to the pan. Cook over a gentle heat for 3–4 minutes, stirring frequently, then return the chicken to the pan. Add the stock, cinnamon stick, paprika and season well with salt and pepper. Bring the soup to the boil, cover and simmer for 1 hour until the vegetables are very tender.

3 While the soup is cooking, blend the saffron in 30ml/2 tbsp boiling water. Beat the egg yolks with the lemon juice in a separate bowl and add the chopped coriander and parsley. When the saffron water has cooled, stir into the egg and lemon mixture.

4 When the vegetables are tender, transfer the chicken to a plate. Spoon away any excess fat from the soup, then increase the heat a little and stir in the vermicelli. Cook for 5–6 minutes until the noodles are tender.

5 Meanwhile, remove the skin from the chicken and, if liked, bone and chop into bite-size pieces. If you prefer, simply skin the chicken pieces.

6 When the vermicelli is cooked, reduce the heat and stir in the chicken pieces and the egg, lemon and saffron mixture. Cook over a very low heat for 1–2 minutes, stirring all the time. Adjust the seasoning and serve with crusty bread.

NUTRITION NOTES	
Per portion:	
Energy	352kcals/1482kJ
Protein	24.3g
Fat	14.6g
Saturated Fat	4.3g
Carbohydrate	33.1g
Fibre	2.5g
Sugars	3.5g
Calcium	53.3mg

Hot-and-sour Soup

This spicy, warming Chinese soup really whets the appetite and is the perfect introduction to a simple meal. Add more vegetables and stock and you can serve it as a main course.

INGREDIENTS

Serves 4

10g/¼ oz dried cloud ears
8 fresh shiitake mushrooms
75g/3oz bean curd (tofu)
50g/2oz/½ cup sliced, drained, canned bamboo shoots
900ml/1½ pints/3¾ cups vegetable stock
15ml/1 tbsp caster sugar
45ml/3 tbsp rice vinegar
15ml/1 tbsp light soy sauce
1.5ml/¼ tsp chilli oil
2.5ml/½ tsp salt
large pinch of ground white pepper
15ml/1 tbsp cornflour
15ml/1 tbsp cold water
1 egg white
5ml/1 tsp sesame oil
2 spring onions, cut into fine rings

1 Soak the cloud ears in hot water for 30 minutes or until soft. Drain, trim off and discard the hard base from each and chop the cloud ears roughly.

2 Remove and discard the stalks from the shiitake mushrooms. Cut the caps into thin strips. Cut the bean curd into 1cm/½in cubes and shred the bamboo shoots finely.

NUTRITION NOTES

Per portion:

Energy	66kcals/276kJ
Protein	4.5g
Fat	2.6g
Saturated Fat	0.4g
Carbohydrate	6g
Fibre	0.5g
Sugars	1.6g
Calcium	109mg

3 Place the stock, mushrooms, bean curd, bamboo shoots and cloud ears in a large saucepan. Bring the stock to the boil, lower the heat and simmer for about 5 minutes.

4 Stir in the sugar, vinegar, soy sauce, chilli oil, salt and pepper. Mix the cornflour to a paste with the water. Add the mixture to the soup, stirring constantly until it thickens slightly.

5 Lightly beat the egg white, then pour it slowly into the soup in a steady stream, stirring constantly. Cook, stirring, until the egg white changes colour.

6 Add the sesame oil just before serving. Ladle the soup into heated bowls and top each portion with spring onion rings.

Hummus

Blending chick-peas with garlic and oil makes a surprisingly creamy purée that is delicious as part of a Turkish-style mezze, or as a dip with vegetables. Leftovers make a good sandwich filler.

INGREDIENTS

Serves 6
150g/5oz/¾ cup dried chick-peas
juice of 2 lemons
2 garlic cloves, sliced
30ml/2 tbsp olive oil
pinch of cayenne pepper
150ml/¼ pint/⅔ cup tahini paste
salt and freshly ground black pepper
extra olive oil and cayenne pepper,
  for sprinkling
flat leaf parsley, to garnish

1 Put the chick-peas in a bowl with plenty of cold water and leave to soak overnight.

2 Drain the chick-peas and cover with fresh water in a saucepan. Bring to the boil and boil rapidly for 10 minutes. Reduce the heat and simmer gently for about 1 hour until soft. Drain.

3 Process the chick-peas in a food processor to a smooth purée. Add the lemon juice, garlic, olive oil, cayenne pepper and tahini and blend until creamy, scraping the mixture down from the sides of the bowl.

4 Season with salt and pepper and transfer to a serving dish. Sprinkle with oil and cayenne pepper and serve garnished with parsley.

— COOK'S TIP —

For convenience, use canned chick-peas. Allow two 400g/14oz cans and drain them well. Tahini paste can be purchased from large supermarkets or health food shops.

NUTRITION NOTES

Per portion:

Energy	270kcals/1126kJ
Protein	105g
Fat	20.2g
Saturated Fat	2.85g
Carbohydrate	12.9g
Fibre	4.7g
Sugars	0.8g
Calcium	210mg

Marinated Vegetable Antipasto

INGREDIENTS

Serves 4

For the peppers
3 red peppers
3 yellow peppers
4 garlic cloves, sliced
handful fresh basil, plus extra to garnish
extra virgin olive oil
salt and freshly ground black pepper

For the mushrooms
450g/1lb open cap mushrooms
60ml/4 tbsp extra virgin olive oil
1 large garlic clove, crushed
15ml/1 tbsp chopped fresh rosemary
250ml/8fl oz/1 cup dry white wine
fresh rosemary sprigs, to garnish

For the olives
1 dried red chilli, crushed
grated rind of 1 lemon
120ml/4fl oz/½ cup olive oil
225g/8oz/1⅓ cups Italian black olives
30ml/2 tbsp chopped fresh parsley
1 lemon wedge, to serve

1 Grill the peppers until they are blackened all over. Remove from the heat and place in a plastic bag. When cool, peel off the skin, halve the peppers and remove the seeds.

2 Cut the flesh into strips lengthways and place them in a bowl with the sliced garlic and basil leaves. Add salt, to taste, cover with oil and marinate for 3–4 hours before serving, tossing occasionally. When serving, garnish with more basil leaves.

3 Thickly slice the mushrooms and place in a large bowl. Heat the oil in a pan, add the garlic and rosemary, then pour in the wine. Simmer for 3 minutes. Add salt and pepper to taste.

4 Pour the mixture over the mushrooms. Mix well and leave until cool, stirring occasionally. Cover and marinate overnight. Serve at room temperature with rosemary sprigs.

5 Prepare the olives. Place the chilli and lemon rind in a small pan with the oil. Heat for about 3 minutes. Add the olives and heat for 1 minute more.

6 Tip into a bowl and leave to cool. Marinate overnight. Sprinkle the parsley over just before serving. Serve garnished with a wedge of lemon.

NUTRITION NOTES	
Per portion:	
Energy	629kcals/2600kJ
Protein	5g
Fat	58.5g
Saturated Fat	8.4g
Carbohydrate	11.6g
Fibre	5.7g
Sugars	9.8g
Calcium	77.3mg

Tuna Carpaccio

Fillet of beef is most often used for carpaccio, but meaty fish like tuna – and swordfish – make an unusual change. The secret is to slice the raw fish wafer thin, made possible by freezing the fish first, a technique used by the Japanese for making sashimi.

INGREDIENTS

Serves 4

2 fresh tuna steaks, about 450g/1lb total weight
60ml/4 tbsp extra virgin olive oil
15ml/1 tbsp balsamic vinegar
5ml/1 tsp caster sugar
30ml/2 tbsp drained bottled green peppercorns or capers
salt and freshly ground black pepper
lemon wedges and green salad, to serve

1 Remove the skin from each tuna steak and place each steak between two sheets of clear film or non-stick baking paper. Pound with a rolling pin until flattened slightly.

2 Roll up the tuna as tightly as possible, then wrap tightly in clear film and place in the freezer for 4 hours or until firm.

3 Unwrap the tuna and cut crossways into the thinnest possible slices. Arrange on individual plates.

4 Whisk together the remaining ingredients, season and pour over the tuna. Cover and allow to come to room temperature for 30 minutes before serving with lemon wedges and green salad.

NUTRITION NOTES

Per portion:

Energy	413kcals/1734kJ
Protein	54.2g
Fat	21.8g
Saturated Fat	4.3g
Carbohydrate	1.6g
Fibre	0
Sugars	1.6g
Calcium	69mg

COOK'S TIP

Raw fish is safe to eat as long as it is very fresh, so check with your fishmonger before purchase, and make and serve carpaccio on the same day. Do not buy fish that has been frozen and thawed.

Pepper Gratin

Serve this simple but delicious dish as a starter with a small watercress, rocket or spinach salad and some good crusty bread to top up the calcium quantity.

INGREDIENTS

Serves 4

2 red peppers
30ml/2 tbsp extra virgin olive oil
60ml/4 tbsp fresh white breadcrumbs
1 garlic clove, finely chopped
5ml/1 tsp drained bottled capers
8 stoned black olives, roughly chopped
15ml/1 tbsp chopped fresh oregano
15ml/1 tbsp chopped fresh
    flat leaf parsley
salt and freshly ground black pepper
fresh herbs, to garnish

1 Preheat the oven to 200°C/400°F/ Gas 6. Place the peppers under a hot grill. Turn occasionally until they are blackened and blistered all over. Remove from the heat and place in a plastic bag. Seal and leave to cool.

2 When cool, peel the peppers. (Don't skin them under the tap, as the water would wash away some of the delicious smoky flavour.) Halve and remove the seeds, then cut the flesh into large strips.

3 Use a little of the olive oil to grease a small baking dish. Arrange the pepper strips in the dish.

NUTRITION NOTES	
Per portion:	
Energy	63kcals/268kJ
Protein	2.1g
Fat	1.3g
Saturated Fat	0.2g
Carbohydrate	11.5g
Fibre	1.5g
Sugars	3.9g
Calcium	32mg

4 Scatter the remaining ingredients on top, drizzle with the remaining olive oil and add salt and pepper to taste. Bake for 20 minutes until the breadcrumbs have browned. Garnish with fresh herbs and serve immediately.

Genoese Squid Salad

This is a good salad for summer, when French beans and new potatoes are at their best. Serve it for a first course or light lunch.

INGREDIENTS

Serves 4

450g/1lb prepared squid, cut into rings
4 garlic cloves, roughly chopped
300ml/½ pint/1¼ cups Italian red wine
450g/1lb waxy new potatoes, scrubbed clean
225g/8oz French beans, trimmed and cut into short lengths
2–3 drained sun-dried tomatoes in oil, thinly sliced lengthways
60ml/4 tbsp extra virgin olive oil
15ml/1 tbsp red wine vinegar
salt and freshly ground black pepper

1 Preheat the oven to 180°C/350°F/ Gas 4. Put the squid rings in an earthenware dish with half the garlic, the wine and pepper to taste. Cover and cook for 45 minutes or until the squid is tender.

2 Put the potatoes in a saucepan, cover with cold water and add a good pinch of salt. Bring to the boil, cover and simmer for 15–20 minutes or until tender. Using a slotted spoon, lift out the potatoes and set aside. Add the beans to the boiling water and cook for 3 minutes. Drain.

3 When the potatoes are cool enough to handle, slice them thickly on the diagonal and place them in a bowl with the warm beans and sun-dried tomatoes. Whisk the oil, wine vinegar and the remaining garlic in a jug and add salt and pepper to taste. Pour over the potato mixture.

4 Drain the squid and discard the wine and garlic. Add the squid to the potato mixture and mix together gently. Serve warm with freshly ground black pepper.

NUTRITION NOTES

Per portion:

Energy	369kcals/1545kJ
Protein	19.7g
Fat	18.2g
Saturated Fat	2.8g
Carbohydrate	20.2g
Fibre	1.3g
Sugars	1.6g
Calcium	29mg

Mussels and Clams with Lemon Grass

Lemon grass has an incomparable flavour and is widely used in Thai cookery, especially with seafood. Coconut cream gives the sauce a creamy consistency. If you have difficulty obtaining the clams for this recipe, use a few extra mussels instead.

INGREDIENTS

Serves 6
1.75kg/4–4½lb mussels
450g/1lb baby clams
120ml/4fl oz/½ cup dry white wine
1 bunch spring onions, chopped
2 lemon grass stalks, chopped
6 kaffir lime leaves, chopped
10ml/2 tsp Thai green curry paste
200ml/7fl oz coconut cream
30ml/2 tbsp chopped fresh coriander
salt and freshly ground black pepper
garlic chives, to garnish

1 Clean the mussels by pulling off the beards, scrubbing the shells well and removing any barnacles. Discard any mussels that are broken or which do not close when tapped sharply. Wash the clams.

2 Put the wine in a large saucepan with the onions, lemon grass, lime leaves and curry paste. Simmer until the wine has almost evaporated.

3 Add the mussels and clams to the pan, cover tightly and steam over a high heat for 5–6 minutes until they open, shaking the pan occasionally. Transfer the mussels and clams to a heated serving bowl and keep hot. Discard any shellfish that remain closed.

4 Strain the cooking liquid into a clean pan and simmer to reduce to about 250ml/8fl oz/1 cup. Stir in the coconut cream and coriander, with salt and pepper to taste. Heat through. Pour the sauce over the mussels and clams and serve, garnished with garlic chives.

NUTRITION NOTES	
Per portion:	
Energy	303kcals/1268kJ
Protein	28.4g
Fat	16.4g
Saturated Fat	10.6g
Carbohydrate	7.7g
Fibre	0.2g
Sugars	3.4g
Calcium	176mg

MEAT AND POULTRY

Packed with flavour, these are the dishes you'll serve again and again,

for family meals, simple suppers or sophisticated dinner parties.

Chicken with Lemon Sauce is a classic that richly deserves its

reputation, while Green Peppercorn and Cinnamon Crusted Lamb is

one of those treats you'll be glad to add to your repertoire. Don't

forget the barbecue: Turkish Kebabs with Tomato and Olive Salsa

and Spicy Indonesian Chicken Satay are sizzling successes.

Green Peppercorn and Cinnamon Crusted Lamb

Racks of lamb are perfect for dinner parties. This version has a spiced crumb coating.

INGREDIENTS

Serves 6
50g/2oz ciabatta bread
15ml/1 tbsp drained green peppercorns
   in brine, lightly crushed
15ml/1 tbsp ground cinnamon
1 garlic clove, crushed
2.5ml/½ tsp salt
25g/1oz/2 tbsp soya
   margarine, melted
10ml/2 tsp Dijon mustard
2 racks of lamb, trimmed
60ml/4 tbsp red wine
400ml/14fl oz/1⅔ cups lamb stock
15ml/1 tbsp balsamic vinegar
fresh vegetables, to serve

1 Preheat the oven to 220°C/425°F/ Gas 7. Break the ciabatta bread into pieces, spread out on a baking sheet and bake for about 10 minutes or until pale golden. Leave to cool, then process the bread in a blender or food processor to make fine crumbs.

2 Tip the crumbs into a bowl and add the green peppercorns, cinnamon, garlic and salt. Stir in the melted soya margarine.

3 Spread the mustard over the lamb. Press the crumb mixture on to the mustard to make a thin, even crust. Put the racks in a roasting tin and roast for 30 minutes, covering the ends with foil if they start to over-brown.

4 Remove the lamb to a carving dish, cover with loosely tented foil and keep hot.

5 Skim the fat off the juices in the roasting tin. Stir in the wine, stock and vinegar. Bring to the boil, stirring in any sediment, then lower the heat and simmer until reduced to a rich gravy. Carve the lamb and serve with the gravy and vegetables.

NUTRITION NOTES

Per portion:

Energy	579kcals/2405kJ
Protein	36.1g
Fat	45.4g
Saturated Fat	22.2g
Carbohydrate	5.2g
Fibre	0.2g
Sugars	0.3g
Calcium	50mg

Pork in Sweet-and-sour Sauce

This recipe is given extra bite with the addition of crushed mixed peppercorns. Served with shelled broad beans tossed with grilled bacon, it is delectable.

INGREDIENTS

Serves 2

1 whole pork fillet, about 350g/12oz
25ml/1½ tbsp plain flour
30–45ml/2–3 tbsp olive oil
250ml/8fl oz/1 cup dry white wine
30ml/2 tbsp white wine vinegar
10ml/2 tsp granulated sugar
15ml/1 tbsp mixed peppercorns,
  coarsely ground
salt and freshly ground black pepper
broad beans tossed with grilled bacon,
  to serve

1 Cut the pork diagonally into thin slices. Place between two sheets of clear film and pound lightly with a rolling pin to flatten them evenly.

2 Put the flour in a shallow bowl. Season well and coat the meat.

— NUTRITION NOTES —	
Per portion:	
Energy	601 kcals/2525KJ
Protein	56.7g
Fat	26.2g
Saturated Fat	18g
Carbohydrate	14.9g
Fibre	0
Sugars	5.5g
Calcium	38mg

3 Heat 15ml/1 tbsp of the oil in a wide heavy-based saucepan or frying pan and add as many slices of pork as the pan will hold. Fry over a medium to high heat for 2–3 minutes on each side until crispy and tender. Remove with a fish slice and set aside. Repeat with the remaining pork, adding more oil as necessary.

4 Mix the wine, wine vinegar and sugar in a jug. Pour into the pan and stir vigorously over a high heat until reduced, scraping the pan to incorporate the sediment. Stir in the peppercorns and return the pork to the pan. Coat the pork with the sauce and heat through. Serve hot with broad beans tossed with grilled bacon.

Chicken with Chianti

Together the full-flavoured, robust red wine and red pesto give this sauce a rich colour and almost spicy flavour, while the grapes add a delicious sweetness. Serve the stew with grilled polenta or warm crusty bread, and accompany with a calcium-rich salad, such as rocket, spinach or watercress, tossed with a fruity flavoured dressing.

INGREDIENTS

Serves 4
45ml/3 tbsp olive oil
4 part-boned chicken breasts, skinned
1 red onion
30ml/2 tbsp red pesto
300ml/½ pint/1¼ cups Chianti
300ml/½ pint/1¼ cups water
115g/4oz red grapes, halved lengthways
    and seeded if necessary
salt and freshly ground black pepper
fresh basil leaves, to garnish
rocket salad, to serve

1 Heat 30ml/2 tbsp of the oil in a large frying pan, add the chicken breasts and sauté over a medium heat for about 5 minutes until they have changed colour on all sides. Remove with a slotted spoon and drain on kitchen paper.

2 Cut the onion in half, through the root. Trim off the root, then slice the onion halves lengthways to create thin wedges.

3 Heat the remaining oil in the pan, add the onion wedges and red pesto and cook gently, stirring constantly, for about 3 minutes until the onion is softened, but not browned.

4 Add the Chianti and water to the pan and bring to the boil, stirring, then return the chicken to the pan and add salt and pepper to taste

5 Reduce the heat, then cover the pan and simmer gently for about 20 minutes or until the chicken is tender, stirring occasionally.

6 Add the grapes to the pan and cook over a low to medium heat until heated through, then taste the sauce for seasoning. Serve the chicken hot, garnished with basil leaves and accompanied by the rocket salad.

WATCHPOINT

Commercial pesto contains Parmesan, which is relatively low in lactose, so most people will find that they can eat this small amount of pesto without causing adverse symptoms. If you'd prefer, make home-made pesto and add grated soya Parmesan instead.

VARIATIONS

Substitute a dry white wine such as pinot grigio for the Chianti, then finish with seedless green grapes. A few spoonfuls of soya cream can be added at the end if you like, to enrich the sauce.

NUTRITION NOTES

Per portion:

Energy	283kcals/1394kJ
Protein	27.8g
Fat	16.8g
Saturated Fat	3.7g
Carbohydrate	5.5g
Fibre	0.4g
Sugars	5.1g
Calcium	65mg

Chicken with Lemon Sauce

Succulent chicken breast fillets with a refreshing lemony sauce and just a hint of lime make a dish that is a sure winner. Serve with stir-fried pak choy or dark green Chinese cabbage.

INGREDIENTS

Serves 4

4 small skinless chicken breast fillets
5ml/1 tsp sesame oil
15ml/1 tbsp dry sherry
1 egg white, lightly beaten
30ml/2 tbsp cornflour
15ml/1 tbsp vegetable oil
salt and ground white pepper
chopped coriander leaves and spring
   onions and lemon wedges, to garnish

For the sauce

45ml/3 tbsp fresh lemon juice
30ml/2 tbsp lime cordial
45ml/3 tbsp caster sugar
10ml/2 tsp cornflour
90ml/6 tbsp cold water

1 Place the chicken breasts in a bowl and add the sesame oil and sherry.

NUTRITION NOTES	
Per portion:	
Energy	349kcals/1460kJ
Protein	42.2g
Fat	9.7g
Saturated Fat	2.7g
Carbohydrate	23.4g
Fibre	0
Sugars	14g
Calcium	17.2mg

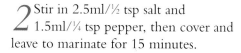

2 Stir in 2.5ml/½ tsp salt and 1.5ml/¼ tsp pepper, then cover and leave to marinate for 15 minutes.

3 Mix together the egg white and cornflour. Add the mixture to the chicken and turn the chicken with tongs until thoroughly coated. Heat the vegetable oil in a non-stick frying pan or wok and fry the chicken fillets for about 15 minutes until the fillets are golden brown on both sides.

4 Meanwhile, make the sauce. Combine all the ingredients in a small pan. Add 1.5ml/¼ tsp salt. Bring to the boil over a low heat, stirring constantly until the sauce is smooth and has thickened slightly.

5 Cut the chicken into pieces and arrange on a warm serving plate. Pour over the sauce, garnish with the coriander leaves, spring onions and lemon wedges and serve.

Fragrant Thai-spiced Chicken Curry

This is perfect for a party as the chicken and sauce can be prepared in advance and combined at the last minute.

INGREDIENTS

Serves 4
45ml/3 tbsp sunflower oil
1 onion, roughly chopped
2 garlic cloves, crushed
15ml/1 tbsp Thai red curry paste
115g/4oz creamed coconut dissolved
    in 900ml/1½ pints/3¾ cups
    boiling water
2 lemon grass stalks, roughly chopped
6 kaffir lime leaves, chopped
150ml/¼ pint/⅔ cup soya yogurt
30ml/2 tbsp apricot jam
1 cooked chicken, about 1.5kg/3–3½lb
30ml/2 tbsp chopped fresh coriander
salt and freshly ground black pepper
kaffir lime leaves, shredded coconut and
    fresh coriander, to garnish
boiled rice, to serve

1 Heat the oil in a saucepan. Add the onion and garlic and fry over a low heat for 5–10 minutes until soft. Stir in the curry paste. Cook, stirring, for 2–3 minutes. Stir in the creamed coconut, then add the lemon grass, lime leaves, soya yogurt and apricot jam. Stir well. Cover and simmer for 30 minutes.

2 Process the sauce in a blender or food processor, then strain it back into a clean pan, pressing as much of the puréed mixture as possible through the sieve.

3 Remove the skin from the chicken, slice the meat off the bones and cut into bite-size pieces. Add to the sauce.

4 Bring the sauce back to simmering point. Stir in the fresh coriander and season with salt and pepper. Serve with rice, garnished with extra lime leaves, shredded coconut and coriander.

COOK'S TIP

If you prefer the sauce a little thicker, stir in a little more creamed coconut after adding the chicken.

NUTRITION NOTES

Per portion:

Energy	667kcals/2786kJ
Protein	61g
Fat	43.2g
Saturated Fat	22.3g
Carbohydrate	9.2g
Fibre	0.3g
Sugars	8.4g
Calcium	39mg

Turkish Kebabs with Tomato and Olive Salsa

INGREDIENTS

Serves 4
2 garlic cloves, crushed
60ml/4 tbsp lemon juice
30ml/2 tbsp olive oil
1 dried red chilli, crushed
5ml/1 tsp ground cumin
5ml/1 tsp ground coriander
500g/1¼lb lean lamb, cut into cubes
8 bay leaves
salt and freshly ground black pepper

For the tomato and olive salsa
175g/6oz/1½ cups mixed pitted green
    and black olives, roughly chopped
1 small red onion, finely chopped
4 tomatoes, peeled and finely chopped
1 red chilli, seeded and finely chopped
30ml/2 tbsp olive oil

1 Mix the garlic, lemon juice, olive
oil, chilli, cumin and coriander in a
large shallow dish. Add the lamb cubes,
with plenty of salt and pepper to taste.
Mix well. Cover and leave to marinate
in a cool place for 2 hours.

2 Make the salsa. Put the olives,
onion, tomatoes, chilli and olive oil
in a bowl. Stir in salt and pepper to
taste. Mix well, cover and set aside.

3 Remove the lamb from the
marinade and divide the cubes
among four skewers, adding the bay
leaves at intervals. Grill over a
barbecue, on a ridged iron grill pan or
under a hot grill, turning occasionally,
for 10 minutes, until the lamb is
browned and crisp on the outside
and pink and juicy inside. Serve with
the salsa.

NUTRITION NOTES	
Per portion:	
Energy	323kcals/1344kJ
Protein	19.3g
Fat	25.9g
Saturated Fat	7.1g
Carbohydrate	4.6g
Fibre	2.5g
Sugars	3.7g
Calcium	54mg

Spicy Indonesian Chicken Satay

INGREDIENTS

Serves 4

4 skinless, boneless chicken breasts,
  about 175g/6oz each
30ml/2 tbsp deep-fried onions

For the marinade

1 fresh red chilli, seeded and
  finely chopped
2 garlic cloves, crushed
60ml/4 tbsp soy sauce
20ml/4 tsp lemon juice

1 Make the marinade by mixing
together the chilli, garlic, soy sauce
and lemon juice. Cut the chicken into
2.5cm/1in cubes, add to the marinade
and mix thoroughly. Cover and leave
in a cool place to marinate for at least
1 hour. Soak eight bamboo skewers in
cold water for 30 minutes.

2 Tip the marinated chicken into a
sieve placed over a saucepan. Leave
to drain for a few minutes. Set the
chicken aside. Add 30ml/2 tbsp hot
water to the marinade and bring to the
boil. Lower the heat and simmer for
2 minutes, then pour into a bowl and
leave to cool. When cool, add the
deep-fried onions.

3 Drain the skewers, thread them
with the chicken and grill or
barbecue for about 10 minutes, turning
regularly until the chicken is golden
brown and cooked through. Serve with
the marinade as a dip.

NUTRITION NOTES	
Per portion:	
Energy	310kcals/1305kJ
Protein	53.7g
Fat	9.4g
Saturated Fat	2.9g
Carbohydrate	2.9g
Fibre	0.4g
Sugars	0.9g
Calcium	23mg

Chicken with Cashew Nuts

An all-time favourite, this classic Chinese dish is delicious served with noodles or rice.

INGREDIENTS

Serves 4
350g/12oz skinless chicken breast fillets
1.5ml/¼ tsp salt
pinch of ground white pepper
15ml/1 tbsp dry sherry
300ml/½ pint/1¼ cups chicken stock
15ml/1 tbsp vegetable oil
1 garlic clove, finely chopped
1 small carrot, cut into cubes
½ cucumber, about 75g/3oz, cut into
   1cm/½in cubes
50g/2oz/½ cup drained canned
   bamboo shoots, cut into cubes
5ml/1 tsp cornflour
15ml/1 tbsp light soy sauce
5ml/1 tsp caster sugar
25g/1oz/¼ cup dry roasted cashew nuts
2.5ml/½ tsp sesame oil
noodles or rice, to serve

1 Cut the chicken into 2cm/¾in cubes. Place the cubes in a bowl, stir in the salt, pepper and sherry, cover and marinate for 15 minutes.

2 Bring the stock to the boil in a large saucepan. Add the chicken and cook, stirring, for 3 minutes. Drain, reserving 90ml/6 tbsp of the stock, and set aside.

3 Heat the vegetable oil in a non-stick frying pan until very hot, add the garlic and stir-fry for a few seconds. Add the carrot, cucumber and bamboo shoots and continue to stir-fry over a medium heat for 2 minutes.

4 Stir in the chicken and reserved stock. Mix the cornflour with the soy sauce and sugar and add to the pan. Cook, stirring, until the sauce thickens slightly, then add the cashew nuts and sesame oil. Toss thoroughly and serve with noodles or rice.

NUTRITION NOTES	
Per portion:	
Energy	243kcals/1016kJ
Protein	29.4g
Fat	10.9g
Saturated Fat	2.5g
Carbohydrate	5.9g
Fibre	0.9g
Sugars	2.9g
Calcium	28mg

Duck with Pineapple

The great thing about Chinese food is that it very rarely contains dairy products, so the dishes make a good choice for a dairy-free diet. The combination of duck, vinegar and pineapple gives this dish a wonderfully subtle sweet-sour flavour.

INGREDIENTS

Serves 4

15ml/1 tbsp dry sherry
15ml/1 tbsp dark soy sauce
2 small skinless duck breasts
15ml/1 tbsp vegetable oil
2 garlic cloves, finely chopped
1 small onion, sliced
1 red pepper, seeded and cut into
   2.5cm/1in squares
75g/3oz/½ cup drained canned
   pineapple chunks
90ml/6 tbsp pineapple juice
15ml/1 tbsp rice vinegar
5ml/1 tsp cornflour
15ml/1 tbsp cold water
5ml/1 tsp sesame oil
salt and ground white pepper
1 spring onion, shredded, to garnish

1 Combine the sherry and soy sauce with plenty of salt and pepper. Lay the duck breasts in a dish, add the marinade, cover and leave for 1 hour.

2 Drain the duck and grill under a medium to high heat for 10 minutes on each side. Cool, then cut into bite-size pieces.

3 Heat the vegetable oil in a non-stick frying pan or wok and stir-fry the garlic and onion for 1 minute. Add the red pepper, pineapple chunks, duck, pineapple juice and vinegar and stir-fry for 2 minutes.

— NUTRITION NOTES —	
Per portion:	
Energy	246kcals/1029kJ
Protein	24.6g
Fat	12.9g
Saturated Fat	3.07g
Carbohydrate	7.1g
Fibre	1.1g
Sugars	4.7g
Calcium	24mg

4 Mix the cornflour to a paste with the water. Add the mixture to the pan with 1.5ml/¼ tsp salt. Cook, stirring, until the sauce thickens. Stir in the sesame oil and serve at once, garnished with spring onion shreds.

FISH AND SHELLFISH

Simplicity is the key to cooking fish. Delicate flavours should be subtly enhanced, not smothered under thick, creamy sauces, so this is one area where you'll never miss milk. When the line-up includes dishes like Monkfish with Tomatoes and Olives, Cajun Blackened Fish with Papaya Salsa or Caribbean Fish Steaks, you can be sure of catching plenty of compliments. Seafood Risotto will also cause quite a stir if you serve it at your next dinner party.

Italian Fish Kebabs

INGREDIENTS

Serves 4

120ml/4fl oz/½ cup olive oil
finely grated rind and juice of
    1 large lemon
5ml/1 tsp crushed chilli flakes
350g/12oz monkfish fillet, cubed
350g/12oz swordfish fillet, cubed
350g/12oz thick salmon fillet, cubed
2 red, yellow or orange peppers, cored,
    seeded and cut into squares
30ml/2 tbsp finely chopped fresh flat
    leaf parsley
salt and freshly ground black pepper

For the sweet tomato and chilli salsa

225g/8oz ripe tomatoes,
    finely chopped
1 garlic clove, crushed
1 fresh red chilli, seeded and chopped
45ml/3 tbsp extra virgin olive oil
15ml/1 tbsp lemon juice
15ml/1 tbsp finely chopped fresh flat
    leaf parsley
pinch of sugar

1 Put the oil in a shallow glass or china bowl and add the lemon rind and juice, the chilli flakes and pepper to taste. Whisk to combine, then add the fish chunks. Turn to coat evenly.

2 Add the pepper squares, stir, then cover and marinate in a cool place for 1 hour, turning occasionally.

3 Thread the fish and peppers on to eight oiled metal skewers, reserving the marinade. Barbecue or grill the fish for 5–8 minutes, turning once.

4 Meanwhile, make the salsa by mixing the ingredients and seasoning to taste with salt and pepper.

5 Heat the reserved marinade, then remove from the heat and stir in the parsley, with salt and pepper to taste. Serve the kebabs hot with the marinade, accompanied by the salsa.

NUTRITION NOTES	
Per portion:	
Energy	621kcals/2586kJ
Protein	48.9g
Fat	44.0g
Saturated Fat	6.9g
Carbohydrate	7.8g
Fibre	2.2g
Sugars	0.2g
Calcium	56mg

Fish Boulettes in Hot Tomato Sauce

This is an unusual and flavoursome dish that needs scarcely any preparation and produces very little washing up, as it is all cooked in one pan. It serves four people as a main course, but also makes a great starter for eight.

INGREDIENTS

Serves 4

675g/1½lb cod, haddock or sea
    bass fillets
pinch of saffron
½ bunch flat leaf parsley
1 egg
25g/1oz/½ cup white breadcrumbs
25ml/1½ tbsp olive oil
15ml/1 tbsp lemon juice
salt and freshly ground black pepper
fresh flat leaf parsley and lemon wedges,
    to garnish

For the sauce

1 onion, very finely chopped
2 garlic cloves, crushed
6 tomatoes, peeled, seeded
    and chopped
1 green or red chilli, seeded and
    finely sliced
90ml/6 tbsp olive oil
150ml/¼ pint/⅔ cup water
15ml/1 tbsp lemon juice

```
              NUTRITION NOTES
  Per portion:
  Energy            240kcals/997kJ
  Protein                     4.8g
  Fat                          21g
  Saturated Fat               3.3g
  Carbohydrate                8.7g
  Fibre                       1.9g
  Sugars                      5.2g
  Calcium                    41mg
```

1 Skin the fish and, if necessary, remove any bones. Cut the fish into large chunks and place in a blender or a food processor.

2 Dissolve the saffron in 30ml/2 tbsp boiling water and pour into the blender or food processor with the parsley, egg, breadcrumbs, olive oil and lemon juice. Season well with salt and pepper and process for 10–20 seconds until the fish is finely chopped and all the ingredients are combined.

3 Mould the mixture into small balls about the size of walnuts and place them in a single layer on a plate.

4 To make the sauce, place the onion, garlic, tomatoes, chilli, olive oil and water in a saucepan. Bring to the boil and then simmer, partially covered, for 10–15 minutes until the sauce is slightly reduced.

5 Add the lemon juice, then place the fish balls in the simmering sauce. Cover and simmer very gently for 12–15 minutes until the fish balls are cooked through. Serve immediately, garnished with flat leaf parsley and lemon wedges.

Seafood Risotto

Risotto is one of Italy's most popular rice dishes and it is made with everything from fresh diced pumpkin to squid ink. On the Mediterranean shores, seafood is the most obvious addition.

INGREDIENTS

Serves 4
60ml/4 tbsp sunflower oil
1 onion, chopped
2 garlic cloves, crushed
225g/8oz/generous 1 cup arborio rice
105ml/7 tbsp white wine
1.5 litres/2½ pints/6¼ cups hot
 fish stock
350g/12oz mixed seafood, such as raw
 prawns, mussels, squid rings or clams
grated rind of ½ lemon
30ml/2 tbsp tomato purée
15ml/1 tbsp chopped fresh parsley
salt and freshly ground black pepper

1 Heat the oil in a heavy-based pan, add the onion and garlic and cook until soft. Add the rice and stir to coat the grains with oil. Add the wine and cook over a moderate heat, stirring, for a few minutes until absorbed.

2 Add 150ml/¼ pint/⅔ cup of the hot stock and cook, stirring constantly, until the liquid is absorbed by the rice. Continue stirring and adding stock in 150ml/¼ pint/⅔ cup quantities, until half is left. This should take about 10 minutes.

3 Stir in the seafood and cook for 2–3 minutes. Add the remaining stock as before, and continue cooking until the rice is creamy and the grains *al dente*.

4 Stir in the lemon rind, tomato purée and parsley. Season with salt and pepper and serve warm.

— NUTRITION NOTES —		
Per portion:		
Energy	438kcals/	1843kJ
Protein		22.4g
Fat		15.4g
Saturated Fat		2.1g
Carbohydrate		51.3g
Fibre		0.8g
Sugars		3.5g
Calcium		70mg

Italian Prawn Skewers

Crunchy crumb-coated prawns make a delicious starter, or serve as a light lunch with a crisp green salad and warm ciabatta bread.

INGREDIENTS

Serves 4
900g/2lb raw tiger prawns, peeled
60ml/4 tbsp olive oil
45ml/3 tbsp vegetable oil
75g/3oz/1¼ cups very fine dry
 ciabatta breadcrumbs
1 garlic clove, crushed
15ml/1 tbsp chopped fresh parsley
salt and freshly ground black pepper
lemon wedges, to serve

1 Slit the prawns down their backs and remove the dark vein. Rinse the prawns in cold water and pat dry using kitchen paper

2 Put the olive oil and vegetable oil in a large bowl and add the prawns, mixing them to coat evenly. Add the breadcrumbs, garlic and parsley and season with salt and pepper. Toss the prawns thoroughly, to give them an even coating of breadcrumbs. Cover and leave to marinate for 1 hour.

— NUTRITION NOTES —	
Per portion:	
Energy	387kcals/1619kJ
Protein	41.4g
Fat	20.4g
Saturated Fat	2.9g
Carbohydrate	9.8g
Fibre	0.5g
Sugars	0.6g
Calcium	204mg

3 Thread the prawns on to four metal or wooden skewers, curling them up as you do so, so that the tail is skewered in the middle

4 Preheat the grill. Place the skewers in the grill pan and cook for about 2 minutes on each side, until the breadcrumbs are golden. Serve with lemon wedges.

Pan-fried Red Mullet with Basil and Citrus

Red mullet is popular all over the Mediterranean. This Italian recipe combines it with oranges and lemons, which grow in abundance in the area.

INGREDIENTS

Serves 4

4 red mullet, about 225g/8oz
  each, filleted
90ml/6 tbsp olive oil
10 peppercorns, crushed
2 oranges, one peeled and sliced and
  one squeezed
1 lemon
30ml/2 tbsp plain flour
15g/½oz/1 tbsp soya margarine
2 drained canned anchovies, chopped
60ml/4 tbsp shredded fresh basil
salt and freshly ground black pepper

1 Place the fish fillets in a shallow dish in a single layer. Pour over the olive oil and sprinkle with the crushed peppercorns. Lay the orange slices on top of the fish. Cover the dish, and leave to marinate for at least 4 hours.

2 Halve the lemon. Remove the skin and pith from one half using a small sharp knife, and slice thinly. Squeeze the juice from the other half.

3 Lift the fish out of the marinade, and pat dry on kitchen paper. Reserve the marinade and orange slices. Season the fish with salt and pepper and dust lightly with flour.

4 Heat 45ml/3 tbsp of the marinade in a frying pan. Add the fish and fry for 2 minutes on each side. Remove from the pan and keep warm.

5 Discard the marinade left in the pan. Melt the soya margarine with any of the remaining original marinade. Cook the anchovies until softened. Stir in the orange and lemon juice, then check the seasoning and simmer until slightly reduced. Stir in the basil. Pour the sauce over the fish and garnish with the reserved orange and lemon slices.

COOK'S TIP

If you prefer, use other fish fillets for this dish, such as lemon sole, haddock or hake.

NUTRITION NOTES	
Per portion:	
Energy	507kcals/2121kJ
Protein	44.9g
Fat	31.5g
Saturated Fat	4.7g
Carbohydrate	11.9g
Fibre	5g
Sugars	6.3g
Calcium	204mg

Cajun Blackened Fish with Papaya Salsa

This is an excellent way of cooking fish, leaving it moist in the middle and crisp and spicy on the outside. The hot, fresh salsa makes a delicious alternative to creamy sauces.

INGREDIENTS

Serves 4
1 quantity Cajun spice (see Cook's Tip)
4 × 225–275g/8–10oz skinned fish fillets such as snapper or bream
50g/2oz/¼ cup soya margarine, melted
wedges of lime and coriander leaves, to garnish

For the papaya salsa
1 papaya
½ small red onion, diced
1 fresh red chilli, seeded and finely chopped
45ml/3 tbsp chopped fresh coriander
grated rind and juice of 1 lime
salt

1 Make the salsa: halve the papaya, scoop out the seeds, then remove the skin and dice the flesh. Add the onion, chilli, coriander, lime rind and juice, with salt to taste. Mix well.

------ COOK'S TIP ------

To make a Cajun spice mix, combine 5ml/1 tsp each of black pepper, ground cumin, mustard powder, chilli powder, dried oregano and salt with 10ml/2 tsp each of paprika and dried thyme.

2 Preheat a heavy-based frying pan over a medium heat for about 10 minutes. Spread the Cajun spice on a plate. Brush the fish fillets with melted soya margarine, then dip them into the spices until well coated.

3 Place the fish in the hot pan and cook for 1–2 minutes on each side until blackened. Serve with the papaya salsa. Garnish with wedges of lime and coriander leaves.

------ NUTRITION NOTES ------

Per portion:

Energy	352kcals/1482kJ
Protein	54g
Fat	13.9g
Saturated Fat	2.9g
Carbohydrate	2.9g
Fibre	0.7g
Sugars	2.9g
Calcium	118mg

Caribbean Fish Steaks

In this quick and easy recipe, a mixture of fresh and ground spices adds an exotic accent to a tomato sauce for fish.

INGREDIENTS

Serves 4
45ml/3 tbsp oil
6 shallots, finely chopped
1 garlic clove, crushed
1 fresh green chilli, seeded and finely chopped
400g/14oz can chopped tomatoes
2 bay leaves
1.5ml/¼ tsp cayenne pepper
5ml/1 tsp crushed allspice
juice of 2 limes
4 cod steaks
5 ml/1 tsp brown muscovado sugar
10ml/2 tsp angostura bitters
salt

1 Heat the oil in a frying pan. Add the shallots and cook for 5 minutes until soft.

2 Add the garlic and chilli and cook for 2 minutes, then stir in the tomatoes, bay leaves, cayenne pepper, allspice and lime juice, with a little salt to taste.

------ NUTRITION NOTES ------

Per portion:

Energy	261kcals/1103kJ
Protein	38.6g
Fat	9.72g
Saturated Fat	1.6g
Carbohydrate	5.5g
Fibre	0.9g
Sugars	4.9g
Calcium	36mg

3 Cook gently for 15 minutes, then add the cod steaks and baste with the tomato sauce. Cover and cook for about 10 minutes or until the steaks are cooked. Transfer the steaks to a warmed dish and keep hot.

4 Stir the sugar and angostura bitters into the sauce, simmer for about 2 minutes, then pour over the fish. Serve with okra or green beans.

VEGETABLES AND SALADS

Colour and flavour are the keynotes of these superb recipes.

Wonderfully versatile, they can be served singly as starters or teamed

up to make a vegetarian meal. Imagine serving a slice of Potato and

Onion Tortilla accompanied by Broad Beans with Mixed Herbs and

Cauliflower with Tomatoes and Cumin, or inviting friends to

celebrate summer with a simply delicious lunch composed of

Mediterranean Roast Vegetable Salad with Marinated Mushrooms.

Broad Beans with Mixed Herbs

Peeling the broad beans is a bit time-consuming, but well worth the effort, and this dish is so delicious that you won't want to eat broad beans any other way.

INGREDIENTS

Serves 4
375g/12oz frozen broad beans
15g/½oz/1 tbsp soya margarine
4–5 spring onions, sliced
15ml/1 tbsp chopped fresh coriander
5ml/1 tsp chopped fresh mint
2.5–5ml/½–1 tsp ground cumin
10ml/2 tsp olive oil
salt

1 Cook the broad beans in lightly salted boiling water for about 4 minutes, or until tender.

2 Drain and, when cool enough to handle, peel away the outer skin, so you are left with the bright green seed.

3 Melt the margarine in a small pan and gently fry the spring onions for 2–3 minutes. Add the broad beans and then stir in the coriander, mint, cumin and a pinch of salt. Stir in the olive oil and serve immediately.

NUTRITION NOTES	
Per portion:	
Energy	122kcals/513kJ
Protein	7.7g
Fat	5.4g
Saturated Fat	2.4g
Carbohydrate	11.3g
Fibre	6.2g
Sugars	1.5g
Calcium	60mg

Courgettes with Moroccan Spices

This is a delicious way of cooking courgettes. Serve as an accompaniment to lamb tagines or stews, roast meats or chicken. To add extra calcium, sprinkle the courgettes with a generous handful of toasted sesame or sunflower seeds before serving.

INGREDIENTS

Serves 4
500g/1¼lb courgettes
lemon juice and chopped fresh
    coriander and parsley, to serve

For the spicy *charmoula*
1 onion
1–2 garlic cloves, crushed
¼ red or green chilli, seeded and
    finely sliced
2.5ml/½ tsp paprika
2.5ml/½ tsp ground cumin
45ml/3 tbsp olive oil
salt and freshly ground black pepper

1 Preheat the oven to 180°C/350°F/ Gas 4. Cut the courgettes into quarters or eighths lengthways, depending on their size, and place in a shallow ovenproof dish or casserole.

2 Finely chop or coarsely grate the onion and blend with the other *charmoula* ingredients and 60ml/4 tbsp cold water. Pour the *charmoula* over the courgettes. Cover the dish with foil or a lid and cook in the oven for 15 minutes.

3 Baste the courgettes with the *charmoula*, and return to the oven, uncovered, for 5–10 minutes until the courgettes are tender. Sprinkle with lemon juice and fresh coriander and parsley and serve.

NUTRITION NOTES	
Per portion:	
Energy	95kcals/392kJ
Protein	2.4g
Fat	8g
Saturated Fat	1.2g
Carbohydrate	3.4g
Fibre	1.3g
Sugars	2.9g
Calcium	35mg

COOK'S TIP
Buy young courgettes with tender skin – older courgettes may need to be peeled.

Marinated Mushrooms

This Spanish recipe makes a nice change from the French classic, mushrooms à la Grecque. Make this dish the day before you eat it, as the flavour will improve with keeping.

INGREDIENTS

Serves 4
30ml/2 tbsp olive oil
1 small onion, very finely chopped
1 garlic clove, crushed
15ml/1 tbsp tomato purée
50ml/2fl oz/¼ cup dry white wine
2 cloves
pinch of saffron strands
225g/8oz button mushrooms, trimmed
salt and freshly ground black pepper
chopped fresh parsley, to garnish

1 Heat the oil in a pan. Add the onion and garlic and cook until soft. Stir in the tomato purée, wine, 50ml/2fl oz/¼ cup water, cloves and saffron and season with salt and pepper.

2 Bring to the boil, cover and simmer gently for 45 minutes, adding more water if it becomes too dry.

3 Add the mushrooms to the pan, then cover and simmer for a further 5 minutes. Remove from the heat and, still covered, allow to cool, then chill in the fridge overnight. Serve cold, sprinkled with chopped fresh parsley.

— NUTRITION NOTES —	
Per portion:	
Energy	93kcals/383kJ
Protein	1.5g
Fat	7.8g
Saturated Fat	1.1g
Carbohydrate	2.2g
Fibre	0.9g
Sugars	1.5g
Calcium	9.8mg

Potato and Onion Tortilla

One of the signature dishes of Spain, this delicious thick potato and onion omelette is eaten there at all times of the day, hot or cold. Try it hot for supper with fresh tomato sauce and thin, crisp French fries, or cold for lunch with cherry tomatoes or salad.

INGREDIENTS

Serves 4
300ml/½ pint/1¼ cups olive oil
6 large potatoes, peeled and sliced
2 Spanish onions, sliced
6 large eggs
salt and freshly ground black pepper
cherry tomatoes, halved, to serve

1 Heat the oil in a large non-stick frying pan. Stir in the potato, onion and a little salt. Cover and cook gently for 20 minutes until soft.

2 Beat the eggs in a large bowl. Remove the cooked onion and potato from the pan with a slotted spoon and add to the eggs. Season with salt and pepper to taste and mix together gently. Pour off some of the oil, leaving about 60ml/4 tbsp in the pan. (Reserve the leftover oil for other cooking.) Heat the pan again.

3 When the oil is very hot, carefully pour in the egg mixture. Cook for 2–3 minutes until the underside is golden brown and the egg is almost set. Cover the pan with a plate and invert the omelette on to it. Slide it back into the pan and cook for 5 minutes more, or until golden brown underneath and still moist in the middle. Serve hot or cold in wedges, with the cherry tomatoes.

— NUTRITION NOTES —	
Per portion:	
Energy	808kcals/3356kJ
Protein	16.5g
Fat	62.1g
Saturated Fat	10.1g
Carbohydrate	48.7g
Fibre	4g
Sugars	4g
Calcium	72mg

Cauliflower with Tomatoes and Cumin

This makes an excellent side dish to serve with barbecued meat or fish and makes a delicious alternative to the traditional cheese sauce.

INGREDIENTS

Serves 4

30ml/2 tbsp sunflower or olive oil
1 onion, chopped
1 garlic clove, crushed
1 small cauliflower, broken into florets
5ml/1 tsp cumin seeds
a good pinch of ground ginger
4 tomatoes, peeled, seeded
   and quartered
15–30ml/1–2 tbsp lemon juice
30ml/2 tbsp chopped fresh
   coriander (optional)
salt and freshly ground black pepper

1 Heat the oil in a cast iron pan, add the onion and garlic and stir-fry for 2–3 minutes until the onion is softened. Add the cauliflower and stir-fry for a further 2–3 minutes until the cauliflower is flecked with brown. Add the cumin seeds and ginger, fry briskly for 1 minute, and then add the tomatoes, 175ml/6fl oz/¾ cup water and some salt and pepper.

— NUTRITION NOTES —	
Per portion:	
Energy	88kcals/366kJ
Protein	2.9g
Fat	6g
Saturated Fat	0.9g
Carbohydrate	5.9g
Fibre	2.1g
Sugars	5g
Calcium	22mg

2 Bring to the boil and then reduce the heat. Cover the pan with a plate or foil and simmer for 6–7 minutes, until the cauliflower is just tender. Don't overcook the cauliflower or it will start to disintegrate.

3 Stir in a little lemon juice to sharpen the flavour, and adjust the seasoning. Scatter over the chopped coriander, if using, and serve at once.

Mediterranean Roast Vegetable Salad

Oven roasting brings out all the flavours of these classic Mediterranean vegetables. Serve them hot or cold with roast, grilled or barbecued meat or fish.

INGREDIENTS

Serves 4

2–3 courgettes
1 Spanish onion
2 red peppers
16 cherry tomatoes
2 garlic cloves, chopped
pinch of cumin seeds
5ml/1 tsp fresh thyme or 4–5 torn
   basil leaves
60ml/4 tbsp olive oil
juice of ½ lemon
5–10ml/1–2 tsp harissa or
   Tabasco sauce
fresh thyme sprigs, to garnish

1 Preheat the oven to 220°C/425°F/ Gas 7. Top and tail the courgettes and cut into long strips. Cut the onion into thin wedges. Cut the peppers into chunks, discarding the seeds and core.

2 Place the vegetables in a cast iron dish or roasting tin, add the tomatoes, chopped garlic, cumin seeds and thyme or basil. Sprinkle with the olive oil and toss to coat.

3 Bake for 25–30 minutes, stirring and turning the vegetables occasionally until they are soft and slightly charred.

4 Blend the lemon juice with the harissa or Tabasco sauce and stir into the vegetables. Serve warm or cold, garnished with the thyme.

— NUTRITION NOTES —	
Per portion:	
Energy	152kcals/631kJ
Protein	2.3g
Fat	11.9g
Saturated Fat	1.8g
Carbohydrate	9.6g
Fibre	2.4g
Sugars	8.4g
Calcium	30mg

Spinach with Beans, Raisins and Pine Nuts

This Mediterranean dish is traditionally made with chick-peas, but can be made with haricot beans as here.

INGREDIENTS

Serves 4

115g/4oz/scant ¾ cup haricot beans
  soaked overnight, or 400g/14oz
  can, drained
60ml/4 tbsp olive oil
1 thick slice white bread
1 onion, chopped
3–4 tomatoes, peeled, seeded
  and chopped
2.5ml/½ tsp ground cumin
450g/1lb spinach
5ml/1 tsp paprika
1 garlic clove, halved
25g/1oz/3 tbsp raisins
25g/1oz/¼ cup pine nuts, toasted
salt and freshly ground black pepper
bread, to serve

1 Simmer the dried haricot beans in clean water for about 1 hour until tender. Drain.

2 Heat 30ml/2 tbsp of the oil in a frying pan and fry the bread until golden. Transfer to a plate.

3 Fry the onion in a further 15ml/ 1 tbsp of the oil over a gentle heat until soft but not brown, then add the tomatoes and cumin and continue cooking over a gentle heat.

4 Wash the spinach thoroughly, removing any tough stalks. Heat the remaining oil in a large pan, stir in the paprika and then add the spinach and 45ml/3 tbsp water. Cover and cook for a few minutes until the spinach has wilted.

5 Add the onion and tomato mixture to the spinach and stir in the beans, then season with salt and pepper.

6 Place the garlic and fried bread in a food processor and blend until smooth. Stir into the spinach and bean mixture, together with the raisins. Add 175ml/6fl oz/¾ cup water and then cover and simmer very gently for 20–30 minutes, adding more water if necessary.

7 Place the spinach on a warmed serving plate and scatter with toasted pine nuts. Serve hot with bread.

NUTRITION NOTES

Per portion:

Energy	372kcals/1352kJ
Protein	12.5g
Fat	17.6g
Saturated Fat	2.4g
Carbohydrate	30.5g
Fibre	9.2g
Sugars	9.5g
Calcium	279mg

Spanish Salad with Capers and Olives

Make this refreshing salad in the summer when tomatoes are sweet and full of flavour.

INGREDIENTS

Serves 4
4 tomatoes
½ cucumber
1 bunch spring onions
1 bunch watercress, washed
8 pimiento-stuffed olives
30ml/2 tbsp drained capers

For the dressing
30ml/2 tbsp red wine vinegar
5ml/1 tsp paprika
2.5ml/½ tsp ground cumin
1 garlic clove, crushed
75ml/5 tbsp olive oil
salt and freshly ground black pepper

1 Peel the tomatoes: place them in a heatproof bowl, add boiling water to cover and leave for 1 minute. Lift out with a slotted spoon and plunge into a bowl of cold water. Leave for 1 minute, then drain. Slip the skins off the tomatoes and dice the flesh finely. Put in a salad bowl.

NUTRITION NOTES

Per portion:

Energy	157kcals/652kJ
Protein	3.5g
Fat	14.2g
Saturated Fat	2.1g
Carbohydrate	4.1g
Fibre	2.5g
Sugars	4g
Calcium	131mg

COOK'S TIP

You can prepare the salad and dressing well ahead, but don't add the dressing until you are ready to serve. Remember to whisk the dressing again to blend the ingredients just before you add it to the salad.

2 Peel the cucumber, dice it finely and add it to the tomatoes. Trim and chop half the spring onions, add them to the salad bowl and mix lightly.

3 Break the watercress into small sprigs. Add to the tomato mixture, with the olives and capers.

4 Make the dressing. Mix the wine vinegar, paprika, cumin and crushed garlic in a bowl. Whisk in the oil and add salt and pepper to taste. Pour the dressing over the salad and toss lightly. Serve at once, with the remaining spring onions.

Fennel, Orange and Rocket Salad

This light and refreshing salad is ideal to serve with very spicy or rich foods.

INGREDIENTS

Serves 4
2 oranges
1 fennel bulb
115g/4oz rocket leaves
50g/2oz/⅓ cup black olives

For the dressing
30ml/2 tbsp extra virgin olive oil
15ml/1 tbsp balsamic vinegar
1 small garlic clove, crushed
salt and freshly ground black pepper

1 With a vegetable peeler, cut strips of rind from the oranges, leaving the pith behind, then cut into thin julienne strips. Cook in boiling water for a few minutes. Drain and set aside.

2 Peel the oranges, removing all the white pith. Slice them into thin rounds and discard any seeds.

3 Cut the fennel bulb in half lengthways and slice across the bulb as thinly as possible, preferably in a food processor fitted with a slicing disc or using a mandoline.

4 Combine the oranges and fennel in a serving bowl and toss with the rocket leaves.

5 Make the dressing; mix together the oil, vinegar, garlic and seasoning. Pour over the salad, toss well and leave to stand for a few minutes. Sprinkle with the black olives and reserved julienne strips of orange.

— NUTRITION NOTES —

Per portion:

Energy	102kcals/427kJ
Protein	2.4g
Fat	7.1g
Saturated Fat	1g
Carbohydrate	7.5g
Fibre	3.4g
Sugars	7.2g
Calcium	105mg

— VARIATION —

Baby spinach leaves or watercress could be used in place of some or all of the rocket, and scatter over a handful of toasted flaked almonds to add some extra calcium.

Aubergine, Lemon and Caper Salad

This cooked vegetable relish is delicious served as an accompaniment to cold meats, with pasta or simply on its own with some good crusty bread. Make sure the aubergine is well cooked until it is meltingly soft.

INGREDIENTS

Serves 4
1 large aubergine, about 675g/1½lb
60ml/4 tbsp extra virgin olive oil
grated rind and juice of 1 lemon
30ml/2 tbsp capers, rinsed
12 stoned green olives
30ml/2 tbsp chopped fresh flat
  leaf parsley
salt and freshly ground black pepper

1 Cut the aubergine into 2.5cm/1in cubes. Heat the olive oil in a large frying pan and cook the aubergine cubes over a medium heat for about 10 minutes, tossing regularly, until golden and softened. You may need to do this in two batches. Drain on kitchen paper and sprinkle with a little salt.

2 Place the aubergine cubes in a large serving bowl, toss with the lemon rind and juice, capers, olives and chopped parsley and season well with salt and pepper. Serve at room temperature.

— NUTRITION NOTES —

Per portion:

Energy	137kcals/567kJ
Protein	1.7g
Fat	12.9g
Saturated Fat	1.9g
Carbohydrate	3.8g
Fibre	3.8g
Sugars	3.4g
Calcium	30mg

PASTA AND GRAINS

Quick, easy and supremely satisfying, pasta and grains are a gift to

the busy cook. More good news is that many of the recipes in this

chapter can be made with ingredients you are likely to have in your

store cupboard, or can find in your local corner shop. Impromptu

meals need never be a problem when you can rustle up

Chilli, Tomato and Olive Pasta or Vegetable and Egg Noodle

Ribbons, while Spicy Paella makes a perfect party piece.

Chilli, Tomato and Olive Pasta

The sauce for this pasta packs a punch, thanks to the robust flavours of red chillies, anchovies and capers.

INGREDIENTS

Serves 4
45ml/3 tbsp olive oil
2 garlic cloves, crushed
2 fresh red chillies, seeded and chopped
6 drained canned anchovy fillets
675g/1½lb ripe tomatoes, peeled, seeded and chopped
2 tbsp sun-dried tomato purée
2 tbsp drained capers
115g/4oz/1 cup pitted black olives, roughly chopped
350g/12oz/3 cups penne
salt and freshly ground black pepper
chopped fresh basil, to garnish

1 Heat the oil in a saucepan and gently fry the garlic and chilli for 2–3 minutes. Add the anchovies, mashing them with a fork, then stir in the tomatoes, sun-dried tomato purée, capers and olives. Add salt and pepper to taste. Simmer gently, uncovered, for 20 minutes, stirring occasionally.

2 Meanwhile, bring a large pan of lightly salted water to the boil and cook the penne according to the instructions on the packet, or until *al dente*. Drain the pasta well and immediately stir into the sauce. Mix thoroughly, tip into a heated serving dish, garnish with chopped fresh basil and serve at once.

NUTRITION NOTES	
Per portion:	
Energy	482kcals/2036kJ
Protein	16.4g
Fat	15.7g
Saturated Fat	1.9g
Carbohydrate	73g
Fibre	5.5g
Sugars	8.4g
Calcium	100mg

Spaghettini with Garlic and Olive Oil

Fresh chilli adds a fiery touch to this simple Italian pasta dish. The cheese that is scattered over the top isn't essential, but adds a delicious salty tang. Use a hard sheep's milk cheese, such as pecorino if you're only allergic to cow's milk, or substitute a soya-based Parmesan cheese.

INGREDIENTS

Serves 4
350g/12oz spaghettini
75ml/5 tbsp extra virgin olive oil
3 garlic cloves, finely chopped
1 fresh red chilli, seeded and chopped
75g/3oz/1½ cups drained sun-dried tomatoes in oil, chopped
30ml/2 tbsp chopped fresh parsley
salt and freshly ground black pepper
freshly grated pecorino cheese, to serve

1 Bring a large saucepan of lightly salted water to the boil. Add the pasta and cook according to the instructions on the packet until *al dente*.

2 Towards the end of the cooking time, heat the oil in a second large pan. Add the garlic and chilli and cook gently for 2–3 minutes. Stir in the tomatoes and remove from the heat.

3 Drain the pasta thoroughly and add it to the hot oil.

4 Return the pan to the heat and cook for 2–3 minutes, tossing the pasta to coat the strands in the sauce. Season with salt and pepper, stir in the parsley and transfer to a warmed serving bowl. Scatter with grated pecorino cheese and serve.

NUTRITION NOTES	
Per portion:	
Energy	554kcals/2325kJ
Protein	11.5g
Fat	28.1g
Saturated Fat	3.9g
Carbohydrate	68g
Fibre	3.1g
Sugars	2.5g
Calcium	38mg

Vegetable and Egg Noodle Ribbons

Serve this elegant, colourful dish with stir-fried broccoli and some crusty bread as a light lunch or as a starter for six to eight people.

INGREDIENTS

Serves 4

1 large carrot, peeled
2 courgettes
50g/2oz soya margarine
15ml/1 tbsp olive oil
6 fresh shiitake mushrooms,
    finely sliced
50g/2oz frozen peas, thawed
350g/12oz broad egg ribbon noodles
10ml/2 tsp chopped mixed herbs, such
    as marjoram, chives and basil
salt and freshly ground black pepper

1 Using a vegetable peeler, carefully slice thin strips from the carrot and from the courgettes.

2 Heat the soya margarine with the olive oil in a large frying pan. Stir in the carrot and shiitake mushrooms; fry for 2 minutes. Add the courgettes and peas and stir-fry until the courgettes are cooked, but still crisp. Season with salt and pepper.

3 Meanwhile, cook the noodles in a large saucepan of boiling water until just tender. Drain the noodles well and tip them into a bowl. Add the vegetables and toss to mix.

4 Sprinkle over the fresh herbs and season to taste. Serve at once.

NUTRITION NOTES	
Per portion:	
Energy	475kcals/2001kJ
Protein	12g
Fat	18.7g
Saturated Fat	7.3g
Carbohydrate	68.8g
Fibre	3.8g
Sugars	4.2g
Calcium	46mg

Vegetable Couscous with Saffron and Harissa

INGREDIENTS

Serves 6

30ml/2 tbsp olive oil
450g/1lb lean lamb, cubed
2 chicken breast quarters, halved
2 onions, chopped
350g/12oz carrots, cut into chunks
225g/8oz parsnips, cut into chunks
115g/4oz turnips, cut into chunks
6 tomatoes, peeled and chopped
900ml/1½ pints/3¾ cups chicken stock
good pinch of ginger
1 cinnamon stick
425g/15oz can chick-peas, drained
400g/14oz/2 cups couscous
2 small courgettes, cut into strips
115g/4oz French beans, halved
50g/2oz/½ cup raisins
a little harissa
salt and freshly ground black pepper

1 Heat half the oil in a large saucepan and fry the lamb until browned, stirring. Transfer to a plate with a slotted spoon. Brown the chicken in the same pan and transfer to the plate.

2 Heat the remaining oil, add the onions and fry over a low heat for 3 minutes, stirring, then add the carrots, parsnips and turnips. Cover and cook for 5 minutes, stirring.

4 Skin the chick-peas in a bowl of cold water, rubbing them between your fingers. Discard the skins and drain. Prepare the couscous according to the instructions on the packet.

6 Transfer the chicken to a plate and remove the skin and bone. Spoon 3–4 large spoonfuls of stock into a separate saucepan. Return the chicken to the stew, add the harissa to the separate stock and heat both gently. Pile the couscous on to a serving dish and make a well in the centre. Spoon the stew over the couscous and serve with the harissa sauce.

3 Add the tomatoes, lamb, chicken and stock. Add the ginger and cinnamon, and season to taste. Bring to the boil and simmer gently for 35–45 minutes until the meat is tender.

5 Add the skinned chick-peas, courgettes, beans and raisins to the meat mixture, cover and cook over a low heat for 10–15 minutes until the vegetables are tender.

NUTRITION NOTES	
Per portion:	
Energy	422kcals/1774kJ
Protein	16.2g
Fat	12.5g
Saturated Fat	1.58g
Carbohydrate	65.3g
Fibre	9.6g
Sugars	17.9g
Calcium	154mg

Spicy Paella

INGREDIENTS

Serves 6

2 large boneless chicken breasts
about 150g/5oz prepared squid
8–10 raw king prawns, shelled
325g/10oz cod or haddock fillets
8 scallops, trimmed and halved
350g/12oz raw mussels in shells
250g/9oz/1⅓ cups long grain rice
30ml/2 tbsp sunflower oil
bunch of spring onions, cut into strips
2 small courgettes, cut into strips
1 red pepper, cut into strips
400ml/14fl oz/1⅔ cups chicken stock
250ml/8fl oz/1 cup passata
salt and freshly ground black pepper
coriander, lemon wedges, to garnish

For the marinade

2 red chillies, seeded
good handful of fresh coriander
10–15ml/2–3 tsp ground cumin
15ml/1 tbsp paprika
2 garlic cloves
45ml/3 tbsp olive oil
60ml/4 tbsp sunflower oil
juice of 1 lemon

1 First make the marinade. Blend all the ingredients in a food processor with 5ml/1 tsp salt.

2 Skin the chicken and cut into bite-size pieces. Place in a glass bowl.

3 Slice the squid into rings. Remove the heads and shell the prawns, leaving the tails intact. Skin the fish and cut into bite-size chunks. Place the fish and shellfish (apart from the mussels) in a separate bowl. Divide the marinade between the fish and chicken and stir well. Cover and marinate for 2 hours.

NUTRITION NOTES

Per portion:

Energy	613kcals/2577kJ
Protein	67.4g
Fat	11.9g
Saturated Fat	2.6g
Carbohydrate	58.4g
Fibre	1.9g
Sugars	5.9g
Calcium	109mg

---

4 Scrub the mussels, discarding any that do not close when tapped sharply, and chill until ready to use. Place the rice in a bowl, cover with boiling water and set aside for about 30 minutes. Drain the chicken and fish, and reserve the marinade separately. Heat the oil in a wok or paella pan and fry the chicken pieces for a few minutes until lightly browned.

5 Add the spring onions to the pan, fry for 1 minute and then add the courgettes and red pepper and fry for a further 3–4 minutes until slightly softened. Remove the chicken and then the vegetables to separate plates.

6 Use a spatula to scrape all the marinade into the pan and cook for 1 minute. Drain the rice, add to the pan and stir-fry for 1 minute. Add the chicken stock, passata and reserved chicken, season with salt and pepper and stir well. Bring the mixture to the boil, then cover the pan with a large lid or foil and simmer very gently for 15–20 minutes until the rice is almost tender.

7 Add the reserved vegetables to the pan and place all the fish and mussels on top. Cover again with a lid or foil and cook over a moderate heat for 10–12 minutes until the fish is cooked and the mussels have opened. Discard any mussels that have not opened during the cooking. Serve garnished with fresh coriander and lemon wedges.

Fried Rice with Mushrooms

A tasty rice dish that is almost a meal in itself. Serve with a crisp green cabbage salad.

INGREDIENTS

Serves 4
225g/8oz/1¼ cups long grain rice
15ml/1 tbsp sunflower oil
1 egg, lightly beaten
2 garlic cloves, crushed
175g/6oz/1¼ cups button
 mushrooms, sliced
15ml/1 tbsp light soy sauce
1.5ml/¼ tsp salt
2.5ml/½ tsp sesame oil
cucumber matchsticks, to garnish

1 Rinse the rice until the water runs clear, then drain thoroughly. Place it in a saucepan. Measure the depth of the rice against your index finger, then bring the finger up to just above the surface of the rice and add cold water to the same depth as the rice.

2 Bring the water to the boil. Stir, boil for a few minutes, then cover the pan. Lower the heat to a simmer and cook the rice for 5–8 minutes until all the water has been absorbed. Remove the pan from the heat and, without lifting the lid, leave for another 10 minutes before forking up the rice.

3 Heat 5ml/1 tsp of the sunflower oil in a non-stick frying pan or wok. Add the egg and cook, stirring with a chopstick or wooden spoon until scrambled. Remove and set aside.

4 Heat the remaining sunflower oil in the pan or wok. Stir-fry the garlic for a few seconds, then add the mushrooms and stir-fry for 2 minutes, adding a little water, if needed, to prevent burning.

NUTRITION NOTES	
Per portion:	
Energy	265kcals/1109kJ
Protein	7.4g
Fat	5.5g
Saturated Fat	1g
Carbohydrate	45.8g
Fibre	0.6g
Sugars	0.1g
Calcium	24mg

5 Stir in the cooked rice and cook for about 4 minutes, or until the rice is hot, stirring from time to time. Add the scrambled egg, soy sauce, salt and sesame oil. Cook for 1 minute to heat through. Serve at once, garnished with cucumber matchsticks.

COOK'S TIP

When you cook rice this way, there may be a crust at the bottom of the pan. Simply soak the crust in water for a couple of minutes to break it up, then drain and fry it with the rest of the rice.

DESSERTS AND BAKES

Go on – treat yourself! This chapter is chock-full of delectable

desserts, from Fresh Fruit with Mango Sauce to Citrus Fruit Flambé

with Pistachio Praline and Filo and Apricot Purses. And to prove

cakes aren't taboo on a dairy-free diet, tuck into Nectarine Amaretto

Cake, Hazelnut Cookies or Banana Gingerbread Slices. On a

savoury note, Olive and Oregano Bread and Focaccia are perfect for

serving with soups, salads and vegetable dishes.

Fresh Fruit with Mango Sauce

The bright, flavourful sauce is easy to prepare and turns a simple fruit salad into something very special. Serve with calcium-enriched soya yogurt.

INGREDIENTS

Serves 6

1 large ripe mango, peeled, stoned and chopped
rind of 1 unwaxed orange
juice of 3 oranges
caster sugar, to taste
2 peaches
2 nectarines
1 small mango, peeled
2 plums
1 pear or ½ small melon
juice of 1 lemon
30–55g/1–2oz/2 heaped tbsp wild strawberries (optional)
30–55g/1–2oz/2 heaped tbsp raspberries
30–55g/1–2oz/2 heaped tbsp blueberries
small mint sprigs, to decorate

1 In a food processor fitted with the metal blade, process the large mango until smooth. Add the orange rind, juice and sugar to taste and process again until very smooth. Press through a sieve into a bowl and chill the sauce.

2 Peel the peaches, if liked, then slice and stone the peaches, nectarines, small mango and plums. Quarter the pear and remove the core and seeds, or, if using, slice the melon thinly and remove the peel.

3 Place the sliced fruits on a large plate, sprinkle with the lemon juice and chill, covered with clear film, for up to 3 hours before serving. (Some fruits may discolour if cut too far ahead of time.)

4 To serve, arrange the sliced fruits on individual serving plates, spoon the berries on top, drizzle with a little of the mango sauce and decorate with mint sprigs. Serve the remaining sauce separately.

NUTRITION NOTES	
Per portion:	
Energy	229kcals/997kJ
Protein	4.4g
Fat	0.6g
Saturated Fat	0
Carbohydrate	54.9g
Fibre	4.9g
Sugars	54.7g
Calcium	51g

Figs and Pears in Honey

INGREDIENTS

Serves 4
1 lemon
90ml/6 tbsp clear honey
1 cinnamon stick
1 cardamom pod
2 pears
3 fresh figs, halved

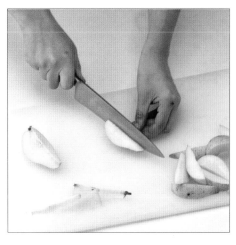

NUTRITION NOTES

Per portion:

Energy	108kcals/465kJ
Protein	0.73g
Fat	0.2g
Saturated Fat	0
Carbohydrate	27.8g
Fibre	2.2g
Sugars	27.8g
Calcium	21mg

1 Pare the rind from the lemon using a zester or vegetable peeler and cut into very thin strips.

2 Place the lemon rind, honey, cinnamon stick, cardamom pod and 350ml/12fl oz/1½ cups water in a pan and boil, uncovered, for about 10 minutes until reduced by about half.

3 Cut the pears into eighths, discarding the core. Leave the peel on or discard as preferred. Place in the syrup, add the figs and simmer for 5 minutes until the fruit is tender.

4 Transfer the fruit to a serving bowl. Continue cooking the liquid until syrupy, then discard the cinnamon stick and pour over the figs and pears.

Fresh Fruit Salad

When peaches and strawberries are out of season, use bananas and grapes, or any other fruits.

INGREDIENTS

Serves 6
2 peaches
2 eating apples
2 oranges
16–20 strawberries
30ml/2 tbsp lemon juice
15–30ml/1–2 tbsp orange
  flower water
icing sugar, to taste
a few fresh mint leaves, to decorate

1 Blanch the peaches for 1 minute in boiling water, then peel away the skin and cut the flesh into thick slices. Discard the stone.

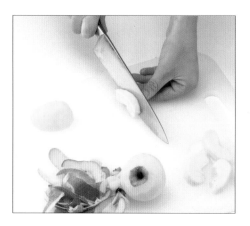

2 Peel and core the apples and cut into thin slices. Peel the oranges with a sharp knife, removing all the pith, and segment them, catching any juice in a bowl.

3 Hull the strawberries and halve or quarter if large. Place all the fruit in a large serving bowl.

4 Blend together the lemon juice, orange flower water and any orange juice. Taste and add a little icing sugar to sweeten, if liked.

5 Pour the fruit juice mixture over the salad and serve decorated with a few fresh mint leaves.

NUTRITION NOTES	
Per portion:	
Energy	79kcals/338kJ
Protein	1.9g
Fat	0.2g
Saturated Fat	0
Carbohydrate	18.5g
Fibre	3.4g
Sugars	18.5g
Calcium	47mg

Dried Fruit Salad with Summer Berries

This is a wonderful combination of fresh and dried fruit and, if you use frozen raspberries or blackberries in the out-of-season winter months, the salad can be made throughout the year. Served with a nutty muesli, it makes a delicious – and calcium rich – breakfast dish.

INGREDIENTS

Serves 4
115g/4oz/½ cup dried apricots
115g/4oz/½ cup dried peaches
1 fresh pear
1 fresh apple
1 fresh orange
115g/4oz/⅔ cup mixed raspberries
  and blackberries
1 cinnamon stick
50g/2oz/¼ cup caster sugar
15ml/1 tbsp clear honey
30ml/2 tbsp lemon juice

1 Soak the apricots and peaches in water for 1–2 hours until plump, then drain and halve or quarter.

2 Peel and core the pear and apple and cut into cubes. Peel the orange with a sharp knife, removing all the pith, and cut into wedges. Place all the fruit in a large saucepan with the raspberries and blackberries.

3 Add 600ml/1 pint/2½ cups water, the cinnamon, sugar and honey.

4 Bring to the boil, then cover the pan and and simmer very gently for 10–12 minutes until the fruit is just tender, stirring occasionally.

5 Remove the pan from the heat and stir in the lemon juice. Allow to cool, then pour the fruit salad into a serving bowl and chill for 1–2 hours before serving.

NUTRITION NOTES	
Per portion:	
Energy	190kcals/811kJ
Protein	2.1g
Fat	0.4g
Saturated Fat	0
Carbohydrate	47.4g
Fibre	5.1g
Sugars	47.4g
Calcium	50mg

Citrus Fruit Flambé with Pistachio Praline

Topping this refreshing citrus fruit dessert with crunchy pistachio praline makes it extra special.

INGREDIENTS

Serves 4
4 oranges
2 ruby grapefruit
2 limes
50g/2oz/¼ cup soya margarine
50g/2oz/⅓ cup light muscovado sugar
45ml/3 tbsp Cointreau
fresh mint sprigs, to decorate

For the praline
oil, for greasing
115g/4oz/½ cup caster sugar
50g/2oz/½ cup pistachio nuts

1 First, make the pistachio praline. Brush a baking sheet lightly with oil. Place the caster sugar and nuts in a small heavy-based saucepan and cook gently, swirling the pan occasionally until the sugar has melted.

2 Continue to cook over a fairly low heat until the nuts start to pop and the sugar has turned a dark golden colour. Pour on to the oiled baking sheet and set aside to cool. Using a sharp knife, chop the praline into rough chunks.

3 Cut off all the rind and pith from the citrus fruit. Holding each fruit in turn over a large bowl, cut between the membranes so that the segments fall into the bowl, with any juice.

4 Heat the soya margarine and muscovado sugar in a heavy-based saucepan until the sugar has melted and the mixture is golden. Strain the citrus juices into the pan and continue to cook, stirring occasionally, until the juice has reduced and is syrupy.

5 Add the fruit segments and warm through without stirring. Pour over the Cointreau and set it alight. As soon as the flames die down, spoon the fruit flambé into serving dishes. Scatter some praline over each portion and decorate with mint sprigs. Serve at once.

NUTRITION NOTES	
Per portion:	
Energy	423kcals/1784kJ
Protein	4.3g
Fat	17.4g
Saturated Fat	7.7g
Carbohydrate	62.5g
Fibre	3.7g
Sugars	62.3g
Calcium	100mg

Apricots Stuffed with Almond Paste

Almonds, whether whole, flaked or ground, have a delightful affinity with apricots.

INGREDIENTS

Serves 6
75g/3oz/scant ½ cup caster sugar
30ml/2 tbsp lemon juice
115g/4oz/1 cup ground almonds
50g/2oz/½ cup icing sugar or
    caster sugar
a little orange flower water (optional)
25g/1oz/2 tbsp melted soya margarine
2.5ml/½ tsp almond essence
900g/2lb fresh apricots
fresh mint sprigs, to decorate

1 Preheat the oven to 180°C/350°F/ Gas 4. Place the sugar, lemon juice and 300ml/½ pint/1¼ cups water in a small saucepan, bring to the boil, stirring occasionally until the sugar has dissolved. Simmer gently for 5–10 minutes to make a thin sugar syrup.

2 Blend the ground almonds with the icing sugar, orange flower water, if using, soya margarine and almond essence to make a smooth paste.

3 Wash the apricots, make a slit in the flesh and ease out the stone. Roll the almond paste into small balls and press one into each apricot.

4 Arrange the stuffed apricots in a shallow ovenproof dish and carefully pour the sugar syrup around them. Cover with foil and bake in the oven for 25–30 minutes.

5 Serve the apricots with a little of the syrup, if liked, and decorate with sprigs of mint.

NUTRITION NOTES

Per portion:

Energy	276kcals/1165kJ
Protein	5.4g
Fat	14.2g
Saturated Fat	1.9g
Carbohydrate	34g
Fibre	3.9g
Sugars	34g
Calcium	70mg

Apple Cake

This moist cake is best served warm. Goat's milk cream whips beautifully and, flavoured with grated lemon, tastes delicious. If you'd prefer, use soya yogurt or soya cream.

INGREDIENTS

Serves 8

675g/1½lb Golden Delicious apples
grated rind and juice of 1 large lemon
4 eggs
150g/5oz/¾ cup caster sugar
150g/5oz/1½ cups plain flour
5ml/1 tsp baking powder
pinch of salt
115g/4oz/½ cup soya margarine,
   melted and cooled, plus extra
   for greasing
1 sachet of vanilla sugar for sprinkling
very finely pared strips of citrus rind,
   to decorate
whipped goat's milk cream, to serve

1 Preheat the oven to 180°C/350°F/ Gas 4. Lightly grease a 23cm/9in springform tin with melted soya margarine and line the base with non-stick paper.

2 Quarter, core and peel the apples, then slice thinly. Put the slices in a bowl and pour over the lemon juice.

3 Put the eggs, sugar and lemon rind in a bowl and whisk with a hand-held mixer until the mixture is thick and mousse-like. When the whisk is lifted out, the mixture should hold it's trail for a few seconds.

4 Sift half the flour, all the baking powder and the salt over the egg mousse, then fold in gently with a large metal spoon. Slowly drizzle in the melted soya margarine from the side of the bowl and fold in gently with the spoon. Sift over the remaining flour, fold in gently, then add the apples and fold these in equally gently.

5 Spoon into the tin and level the surface. Bake for 40 minutes or until a skewer comes out clean. Leave to settle in the tin for about 10 minutes, then invert on a wire rack. Turn the cake the right way up and sprinkle the vanilla sugar over the top. Decorate with the citrus rind. Serve warm, with the goat's milk cream.

— NUTRITION NOTES —	
Per cake:	
Energy	2256kcals/9474kJ
Protein	16.8g
Fat	96.42g
Saturated Fat	28.8g
Carbohydrate	350g
Fibre	15g
Sugars	236.4g
Calcium	246mg

Nectarine Amaretto Cake

Try this delicious cake with soya yogurt for dessert, or serve it solo for afternoon tea.

INGREDIENTS

Serves 4–6
soya margarine, for greasing
3 eggs, separated
175g/6oz/¾ cup caster sugar
grated rind and juice of 1 lemon
50g/2oz/⅓ cup semolina
40g/1½oz/⅓ cup ground almonds
25g/1oz/¼ cup plain flour
2 nectarines, halved and stoned
apricot glaze (see Cook's Tip)

For the syrup
75g/3oz/6 tbsp caster sugar
30ml/2 tbsp Amaretto liqueur

1 Preheat the oven to 180°C/350°F/ Gas 4. Grease a 20cm/8in round loose-based caked tin with a little soya margarine. Whisk the egg yolks, caster sugar, lemon rind and juice in a large bowl until thick. Fold in the semolina, almonds and flour until smooth.

2 Whisk the egg whites in a grease-free bowl until fairly stiff. Using a metal spoon, stir a spoonful of the whites into the semolina mixture, then fold in the remaining egg whites. Spoon the mixture into the prepared cake tin.

3 Bake for 30–45 minutes until the cake springs back when lightly pressed. Loosen the cake around the edge with a palette knife. Prick with a skewer and leave to cool in the tin.

4 Meanwhile, make the syrup. Heat the sugar and 90ml/6 tbsp water in a small pan, stirring until dissolved, then boil without stirring for 2 minutes. Add the Amaretto liqueur and drizzle slowly over the cake.

5 Remove the cake from the tin and transfer it to a serving plate. Slice the nectarines and arrange them over the top. Brush with apricot glaze.

COOK'S TIP

To make apricot glaze, heat 60ml/4 tbsp apricot jam with a squeeze of lemon juice until the jam melts, then sieve.

NUTRITION NOTES

Per cake:

Energy	1980kcals/8382kJ
Protein	41.4g
Fat	43.8g
Saturated Fat	7.8g
Carbohydrate	366g
Fibre	7.8g
Sugars	309g
Calcium	294mg

Filo and Apricot Purses

Filo pastry is very easy to use. Keep a packet in the freezer ready for rustling up a speedy tea-time treat.

INGREDIENTS

Makes 12
115g/4oz/¾ cup ready-to-eat
   dried apricots
45ml/3 tbsp apricot compote
   or conserve
3 macaroons, crushed
3 filo pastry sheets
20ml/4 tsp soya margarine, melted,
   plus extra for greasing
icing sugar, for dusting

—————— COOK'S TIP ——————

The easiest way to crush macaroons is to put them in a sturdy plastic bag and roll lightly with a rolling pin.

1 Preheat the oven to 180°C/350°F/ Gas 4. Lightly grease two baking sheets with a little soya margarine. Chop the apricots, put them in a bowl and stir in the apricot compote or conserve. Add the crushed macaroons and mix well.

2 Cut the filo pastry into 24 x 13cm/ 5in squares, pile the squares on top of each other and cover with a clean dish towel to prevent the pastry from drying out and becoming brittle.

3 Lay one pastry square on a flat surface, brush lightly with melted soya margarine and lay another square on top. Brush the top square with melted margarine. Spoon a small amount of apricot mixture in the centre of the pastry, bring up the edges and pinch together in a money-bag shape. Repeat with the remaining pastry squares and filling to make 12 purses in all.

4 Arrange the purses on the baking sheets and bake for 5–8 minutes until golden brown. Transfer to a wire rack and dust lightly with icing sugar. Serve warm.

—————— NUTRITION NOTES ——————

Per portion:

Energy	58kcals/244kJ
Protein	0.6g
Fat	2.4g
Saturated Fat	0.6g
Carbohydrate	8.8g
Fibre	0.8g
Sugars	7.7g
Calcium	11.5mg

Hazelnut Cookies

Serve these sweet little nut cookies as petits fours with after-dinner coffee – as a healthy bonus, they are rich in calcium.

INGREDIENTS

Makes about 26
115g/4oz/8 tbsp soya margarine
75g/3oz/¾ cup icing sugar
115g/4oz/1 cup plain flour
75g/3oz/¾ cup ground hazelnuts
1 egg yolk
26 blanched hazelnuts, to decorate
icing sugar, for dusting

1 Preheat the oven to 180°C/350°F/ Gas 4. Line 3–4 baking sheets with non-stick baking paper. Cream the soya margarine and sugar together with an electric mixer until light and fluffy.

2 Beat in the flour, ground hazelnuts and egg yolk until evenly mixed.

NUTRITION NOTES

Per cookie:

Energy	102kcals/426kJ
Protein	1.5g
Fat	7.9g
Saturated Fat	1.4g
Carbohydrate	6.7g
Fibre	0.5g
Sugars	3.3g
Calcium	16mg

3 Take a teaspoonful of mixture at a time and shape it into a smooth round with your fingers. Place the rounds well apart on the baking paper and press a whole hazelnut into the centre of each one.

4 Bake the cookies, one tray at a time, for about 10 minutes or until golden brown, then transfer to a wire rack using a palette knife. Sift icing sugar over each cookie to cover. Leave to cool.

Banana Gingerbread Slices

Bananas make this spicy bake delightfully moist. The flavour develops on keeping, so store the gingerbread for a few days before cutting into slices if possible.

INGREDIENTS

Serves 6

soya margarine for greasing
275g/10oz/2½ cups plain flour
5ml/1 tsp bicarbonate of soda
20ml/4 tsp ground ginger
10ml/2 tsp mixed spice
115g/4oz/⅔ cup soft light brown sugar
60ml/4 tbsp sunflower oil
30ml/2 tbsp molasses or black treacle
30ml/2 tbsp malt extract
2 eggs
60ml/4 tbsp orange juice
3 ripe bananas
115g/4oz/⅔ cup raisins

1 Preheat the oven to 180°C/350°F/ Gas 4. Lightly grease and line a 28 x 18cm/11 x 7in shallow baking tin.

2 Sift the flour, bicarbonate of soda and spices into a mixing bowl. Place the sugar in a sieve over the bowl, add some of the flour mixture and rub through the sieve.

3 Make a well in the centre of the dry ingredients and add the oil, molasses or treacle, malt extract, eggs and orange juice. Mix throroughly.

4 Mash the bananas on a plate. Add the raisins to the gingerbread mixture, then mix in the mashed bananas.

5 Scrape the mixture into the prepared baking tin. Bake for about 35–40 minutes or until the centre of the gingerbread springs back when lightly pressed.

6 Leave the gingerbread in the tin to cool for 5 minutes, then turn out on to a wire rack to cool completely. Transfer to a board and cut into 20 slices to serve.

NUTRITION NOTES	
Per cake:	
Energy	2712kcals/11490kJ
Protein	49.2g
Fat	63g
Saturated Fat	10.2g
Carbohydrate	525g
Fibre	13.8g
Sugars	302g
Calcium	942mg

— COOK'S TIP —

If your brown sugar is lumpy, mix it with a little flour and it will be easier to sift.

Olive and Oregano Bread

This is a great accompaniment to salads and is good served warm.

INGREDIENTS

Serves 8-10
300ml/10fl oz/1¼ cups warm water
5ml/1 tsp active dried yeast
pinch of sugar
15ml/1 tbsp olive oil
1 onion, chopped
450g/1lb/4 cups strong white flour
5ml/1 tsp salt
1.5ml/¼ tsp freshly ground
    black pepper
50g/2oz/¼ cup black olives
15ml/1 tbsp black olive paste
15ml/1 tbsp chopped fresh oregano
15ml/1 tbsp chopped fresh parsley

1 Put half the water in a jug. Sprinkle the yeast on top. Mix in the sugar and leave in a warm place for about 10 minutes until frothy.

2 Heat the olive oil in a frying pan, add the onion and fry gently until softened and golden brown.

3 Sift the flour with the salt and pepper. Make a well in the centre. Add the yeast mixture, the fried onion (with the oil), the olives, olive paste, herbs and remaining water. Gradually incorporate the flour and mix, adding a little water if necessary.

4 Turn the dough on to a floured surface and knead until smooth and elastic. Place the dough in a mixing bowl, cover with a damp cloth and leave in a warm place to rise until doubled in bulk. Lightly grease a baking sheet with soya margarine.

5 Turn the dough on to a floured surface and knead again. Shape into a 20cm/8in round and place on the baking sheet. Make criss-cross cuts over the top, cover and leave in a warm place for 30 minutes until well risen. Preheat the oven to 220°C/425°F/Gas 7.

6 Dust the loaf with flour. Bake for 10 minutes, then lower the temperature to 200°C/400°F/Gas 6. Bake for 20 minutes more or until the loaf sounds hollow when it is tapped underneath. Transfer to a wire rack to cool before serving.

NUTRITION NOTES

Per loaf:

Energy	1920kcals/8130kJ
Protein	63g
Fat	41g
Saturated Fat	9g
Carbohydrate	345g
Fibre	15g
Sugars	15g
Calcium	97mg

Focaccia

This makes a delicious snack served warm with low fat cheese and chunks of fresh tomato.

INGREDIENTS

Serves 8
300ml/½ pint/1¼ cups warm water
5ml/1 tsp dried yeast
pinch of sugar
450g/1lb/4 cups strong white flour
5ml/1 tsp salt
1.5ml/¼ tsp freshly ground
  black pepper
15ml/1 tbsp pesto
115g/4oz/⅔ cup stoned black
  olives, chopped
25g/1oz/3 tbsp drained sun-dried
  tomatoes in oil, chopped, plus
  15ml/1 tbsp oil from the jar
5ml/1 tsp coarse sea salt
5ml/1 tsp roughly chopped
  fresh rosemary

1 Put the water in a bowl. Sprinkle the yeast on top. Add the sugar, mix well and leave for 10 minutes. Lightly grease a 33 x 23cm/13 x 9in Swiss roll tin.

2 Sift the flour, salt and pepper into a bowl and make a well in the centre. Add the yeast mixture with the pesto.

3 Stir in the olives and sun-dried tomatoes (reserve the oil). Mix to a soft dough, adding extra water if necessary. Knead the dough on a floured surface for 5 minutes until smooth and elastic. Return to the clean bowl, cover with a damp dish towel and leave in a warm place to rise for about 2 hours, until doubled in bulk.

4 Turn the dough on to a floured surface, knead briefly, then roll out to a 33 x 23cm/13 x 9in rectangle. Lift the dough over the rolling pin and place in the prepared tin. Preheat the oven to 220°C/425°F/Gas 7.

5 Using your fingertips, make small indentations all over the dough. Brush with the reserved oil from the sun-dried tomatoes, then sprinkle with the salt and rosemary. Leave to rise for 20 minutes, then bake for 20–25 minutes, or until golden. Transfer to a wire rack and leave to cool slightly before serving.

NUTRITION NOTES	
Per portion:	
Energy	1176kcals/7517kJ
Protein	35.3g
Fat	34.9g
Saturated Fat	4.9g
Carbohydrate	351.6g
Fibre	13.2g
Sugars	84.9g
Calcium	544mg

INFORMATION FILE

USEFUL ADDRESSES

The British Allergy Foundation
Deepdene House
30 Bellegrove Road
Welling
Kent DA16 3PY
Tel: 0181 303 8525 / 8583
(Helpline 0891 516500)

The British Dietetic Association
7th Floor, Elizabeth House
22 Suffolk Street
Queensway
Birmingham B1 1LS
Tel: 0121 643 5483

The British Nutrition Foundation
High Holborn House
52–54 High Holborn
London WC1V 6RQ
Tel: 0171 404 6504
Fax: 0171 404 6747

The National Eczema Society
163 Eversholt Street
London NW1 1BU
Tel: 0171 388 4097

The National Asthma Campaign (and Junior Asthma Club)
Providence House
Providence Place
London N1 0NT
Tel: 0171 226 2260
(Helpline 0345 010203)

Allergycare
(Mail-order specialist food suppliers)
1 Church Square
Taunton
Somerset TA1 1SA
Tel: 01823 325022/3

The British Goat Society
34–36 Fore Street
Bovey Tracey
Newton Abbott
Devon TQ13 9AD
Tel: 01626 833168

The National Osteoporosis Society
PO Box 10
Radstock
Bath BA3 3YB
Tel: 01761 471771

The Vegan Society
Donald Watson House
7 Battle Road
St Leonards on Sea
East Sussex TN37 7AA
Tel: 01424 427393

FURTHER READING
The Inside Story on Food and Health
Subscription magazine with general information on diet and nutrition.
Available from:
Berrydales Publishers
Berrydale House
5 Lawn Road
London NW3 2XS
Tel: 0171 722 2866

GLOSSARY OF BASIC TERMS

Allergen – a substance in the environment that causes an allergic reaction.

Allergic rhinitis – persistent runny nose, sneezing and watery eyes caused by allergens.

Allergy – the result of the body's immune system (defense mechanism) over-reacting following exposure to normally harmlesss substances.

Atopy – an inherited tendency to suffer from allergies.

Eczema – an allergic reaction of the skin characterised by small blisters which flake and cause extreme itching.

Histamine – one of the major chemicals released by so-called "mast" cells when the immune system is exposed to an allergen, causing an inflammatory reaction.

Lactase – an enzyme found in the small intestine required to digest lactose.

Lactose – a sugar found only in human milk and milk from other animals.

Lactose intolerance – failure to digest lactose due to reduced levels of lactase, causing unpleasant symptoms.

INDEX